TODAY IS THE DAY

IS THE

DAY

THREE KEYS TO LIVING YOUR ULTIMATE LIFE

OBOM A. BOWEN

Today Is the Day
– Three Keys to Living Your Ultimate Life

Published by Today Is the Day Publishing
www.todayisthedaybook.com

All Scripture quotations, unless otherwise indicated, are taken from the Holy Bible, New International Version ®, NIV®. Copyright © 1973, 1978, 1984, 2011 Biblica, Inc ™ Used by permission of Zondervan. All rights reserved worldwide. www.zondervan.com

ISBN 978-1-943157-62-4

Printed in United States of America

For more information:
www.todayisthedaybook.com

"Most people consider themselves or their lives a failure, before they define what success looks like for THEM!"
— Obom Bowen

We hope you enjoy this book from Obom Bowen.

Our goal is to provide high-quality, thought- provoking books, products, and retreats that connect truth to your real needs and challenges.

For more information on other books and products that will help you with all your important life, growth, & relationships go to:
www.TodayIsTheDayBook.com

DEDICATION

This book is truly my life's work and labor of love. With that I dedicate this book to you, the reader. This book is dedicated to every person, young and old, employed and unemployed, educated and uneducated, that dreams of becoming wealthy and building a happy, successful, and rewarding life, but is too intimidated to take that first step. It is the hope and dream of the Bowen family that today is the day for you.

The primary reason I wrote this book is to help men and women know that it's ok not to compromise, to love to the fullest and believe that abundance is possible for you.

Today Is the Day is dedicated to you because, at one point in my life, I researched everything I could about the most important aspects of life: Success, Love, Wealth. Over the last 15 years, I practiced every discipline and held myself accountable to produce this book as a gift to my children, to prepare them for life, love, and fulfillment. So, what you will find as you sink your teeth into this book are some of my favorite and proven methods to date.

My wife and I practice daily, so we can live our own fairytale.

After reading this book, if you would like to continue your journey and join the Manifest Wealth Systems movement with us, I would be honored to continue to serve you. Before I die, my vision is to make an impacting, positive change to ONE Billion Families throughout the world.

WHAT OTHERS ARE SAYING

Today is the Day is absolutely, hands down the best book I have ever read. The amount of information amongst these pages is everything you have ever needed or wanted to change your entire life! From yourself, to relationships, to business, this life-changing information is priceless! Obom Bowen is a remarkable genius with the ability to teach others gracefully through his writing.

The knowledge in this book came at a time in my life when I was searching for answers and lessons to transform my own life. I admire Obom so much for sharing all this knowledge with the rest of the world, as this book has completely taught me to change everything I ever wanted to change! I am excited to continue to read this book over and over for years to come! Obom is a gift to this world and his writing will teach you to transform your own world! *Today is the Day* is beyond inspiring!!!

— Britney Gutzwiller
CEO, Be Bold Be Brave
Author, *The Best and Worst of Post-Partum*

Obom has changed my life drastically since my encounter with him. He has taught me many valuable lessons that have allowed for my mind to grow and lifestyle to enhance for the greater. I have a new sense of faith and confidence as well as strings of successful happy days with the knowing of many more to come. I highly suggest if you are looking for growth, change, and results you consider Obom's teachings and *Today Is the Day* is where you must start.

— Joseph Tomczyk
Founder CEO, Livepositive365

After having read and mastered *Today Is the Day*, you may well discover your potential as you have never before seen it; to find true greatness and abundance. Obom Bowen is a great philosopher, opening your mind with new insights from the age-old Methodologies of the Bible. Both his content and principles form a solid foundation for effective communication. Let the words touch you. Let the message of Obom Bowen inspire you. Allow Obom's philosophy to affect your life.

> — Robert L. Sims
> Author, *The Decisions We Didn't Know We Made*

The information in this book is pure gold!!! It continues to transform me as a person and transform my life in more ways than I can count. The most important lesson by far was learning the true power of my mind and how to create lasting positive change. Learning how to live a life free from "stress" has been the most life changing experience that has led to more peace of mind, creative flow, and the ability to move forward with all my dreams and goals.

The tools and philosophies I've learned have positively impacted every aspect of my life, from creating deeper connections in my relationships, building more clarity and direction in my businesses, and clearing the path for my vision, which in turn, is designing and creating the life of my dreams. Obom Bowen is a true blessing in my life. He is a gift to this world, and I am so excited to see this information getting out to people of all walks of life. *Today Is the Day* will not only change your day, but will change your entire life!!

> — Vicki Colt
> CEO, Rock Your Love
> Author, *Unbounded Love*

ACKNOWLEDGEMENTS

Thank you to my wife, Ana Bowen, for being the greatest love of my life and a true example of love, support, and strength.

A very special thank you to my oldest daughter Iliavah, you taught me how to love deeper and more openly than ever before. This book is my gift to you, to be there in the moments when you would need daddy's advice, but I'm not physically there with you. I love you, sweetheart.

A very special thank you to my younger daughter Iliyhana — you have taught me to be patient and know that God is real and present, even before you were born. This book is my gift to you, to be there in the moments when you would need daddy's advice, but I'm not physically there with you. I love you, sweetheart.

To Vicki Colt, God is not done with you yet. You helped me to remain passionate and LOVE with my heart fully open; you are a true example that learning is a lifetime commitment.

CONTENTS

Before you go any further in this book, my first gift for you is to help you DEFINE what SUCCESS looks like for you. Today is the day for you to define success in these simple but profound areas.

Life:

_____
_____
_____
_____
_____
_____
_____
_____
_____

Relationship:

_____
_____
_____
_____
_____
_____
_____
_____
_____

Work:

_____
_____
_____
_____

_____
_____
_____
_____

Business:

_____
_____
_____
_____
_____
_____
_____
_____
_____

Parenting:

_____
_____
_____
_____
_____
_____
_____
_____
_____

Now that you have an idea, this book will become the instructional manual to your Wealth. CONGRATULATIONS!

PREFACE

The foundation of all human action is human thought. Our thought process forms the foundation on which we build every facet of our lives. Therefore, it is important to understand how our minds work – how we got the habits and attitudes, the beliefs that may stand in the way of releasing our vast inner potential and leading fulfilling and purposeful lives. Our beliefs and expectations about ourselves, our families, our organizations – indeed, our world – are directly reflected in our "performance reality."

Today Is the Day is designed to build your understanding, with a structured process, of how your mind works and how you control the way you think to achieve success – in any part of your life that you desire. Based on decades of research in the field of cognitive psychology, social learning theory, and high achievement, the education presented here stands at the forefront, reflecting the qualities and characteristics of high – performance individuals and organizations.

Vividly presenting the concepts and education in this book, I'll be providing and revealing productive insights into how you think and how your thoughts affect how you act. The tools and techniques I share here, in easily recognizable stories and examples, can be applied immediately to help you reach your goals easily and enjoyably. Life is propelled out of the ordinary and into an exciting adventure.

By participating in this book, you join millions upon millions of people around the world who have discovered that the path to true success lies in their own thinking. From small businesses proprietors to Fortune 500 executives, from clergy to military, from educators to political leaders, the economically devastated and prison inmates, from students to bureaucrats, athletes, healthcare professionals, and tech industries – all are using this information, this education, to make a positive difference in the world around them.

In the early 2000s, after I had been teaching college Psychology for five years while on active duty in the Marine Corps, the director of staff development at one of our state agencies asked me to design and lead a two-day workshop on Social Learning Theory. I called the course "Today Is the Day."

Soon I had requests from other agencies as well, and my client list began to grow. Today, the book is also a business offering a wide range of thinking skills seminars in the workplace. It has developed a reputation for offering the most practical and enlightening programs ever to come out of the fields of cognitive and self–image psychology, social learning theory, and high–achiever research.

Nearly a decade after that first workshop, I started creating human behavioral change and psychological tips and sending them out via email, primarily as a service to clients who wanted to continue honing their growth and achievement skills after they had participated in a Today Is the Day class. After seventeen years of service and teaching at the college level and ten years of conducting seminars in the business arena, I had a pretty good idea about Human Behavior and Psychology, mechanics, and usage issues that trouble individuals most frequently.

The writing tips, I hoped, would clarify some of the confusion many people experience as they began to change. The guiding principle of this book is that individuals have a virtually unlimited capacity for growth, change, and creativity and can adapt readily to the tremendous changes taking place in this fast–paced, technological age. Central to this is the reality that individuals are responsible for their own actions and can relate their behavior through a structured process that includes goal setting, self-reflection, and self-evaluation, among other things.

By applying the *Today Is the Day* education, people are able to develop their potential by changing their habits, attitudes, beliefs, and expectations. This, in turn, allows individuals in an organizational setting to achieve higher levels of growth and productivity, as well as shifting the collective behavior. This shift leads to more constructive organizational cultures and healthier, higher performing workplaces.

We have an unlimited capacity for growth, change, and creativity.

Very early in the process, I enlisted the help of my wife and longtime associate, Ana Bowen, as a Curriculum Advisor. She is scholastically trained in Education and Sociology. Ana and I believe (and teach!) that great change demands rewriting the way we think, and I can assure you that we practice what we preach. Each chapter was drafted and revised by me and then sent to Ana for further revisions and editing, launching a series of volleys between us as we worked to make the information as clear and concise as possible. Not only did she collaborate with me in writing the chapters and teaching our courses, but she also created and executed the design and layout of this book.

Solidly grounded in the latest research from the fields of cognitive psychology and social learning theory, documented results clearly show measurable increases in organizational effectiveness and productivity after applying the Today Is the Day concepts.

So, one might ask, "If the workshops are so good, why did you feel the need to publish this content as a book?"

The initial and primary reason is our students asked for it. Like us, many of them still enjoy the printed book — something they can hold, throw in a briefcase, keep on their desks, lend to a friend, or give as a gift. Web and classroom courses are handy, but they are not as good for reading in bed, in a long line, in a hammock, or at the beach.

Second, like most writers, I was not content to leave well enough alone. I knew that we could strengthen the tips by revising them (again!) and publishing them together as a book, so that gave me a good reason to do so. I have tightened explanations, added examples, deleted examples that were problematic, and even corrected a few outright mistakes (yes, I am human).

Finally, I hope this book will extend learning beyond the limitations of a six-hour seminar or a fourteen-week college semester. Next Level Growth classes, courses, and books such as *Today Is the Day* must first address the larger concerns of gradual transformation which in the end seems almost magical: organization and development, tone and clarity, cognitive and self-image psychology, social learning theory, and high achievement.

Working carefully through those issues leaves little time to talk about the final stage of the transformation. Often, classes are able to focus on social learning theory, high achievement mechanics, and usage for only a short time, covering only the most common errors. Anyone who is serious about effective life change must be committed to ongoing self-improvement and should avail themselves to many resources – and *Today Is the Day* is the best and most comprehensive resource to date.

Finally, I believe excellence is a process – an achievable, continuous process that inevitably results when we learn to control how we think, what we expect, and what we believe. International business, political, and military leaders consult with me on how to do more with less and bring out the best in those with whom they work. Top athletes come to me for help with mastering the psychological aspects of peak performance. I continue to work with educators on strategies that motivate both staff and students to set and achieve meaningful goals. My absolute passion resides in helping others understand and achieve greatness within their lives, businesses, and relationships, going beyond their own self-imposed limitations and beliefs about what or who they believe themselves to be.

We are going to deal with some very powerful material in this book. I'm going to show you how to turn yourself, your business, and your relationships loose in a way you have never been turned loose before. I ask that you do not think of this book as some other book or a workbook. Rather, think of it as an affirmative guide we are co-authoring. Think of this as your MANUAL, your book, your chart, and your guideline to personal, life, business, and relationship growth and excellence, the kind of growth and relationship accomplishment you never believed possible.

What I intend to help you do is to throw away the many invalid conditioned beliefs about yourself or relationships you have. As we work together in this book, you will see how practical this information can be. A whole planned, positive way to enhance your life is open to you. You will not only grow yourself, but you will show the people and other relationships around you how they can grow too. You will learn how to achieve goals you never thought before – personal, relational, family, spiritual, and organizational, whatever you choose. You will learn how to increase your self-efficacy – your ability to make things happen – both personally and professionally, but most importantly in all your relationships.

A wealth of sound psychological material has been condensed here. I have presented it in practical, easy-to-understand concepts. Our basic premise is this: we act, we work, we produce, we behave, not in accordance with the truth, but only with the truth as we perceive it to be. You will see throughout this book and its exercises that if we change the way we think, we can change the way we act.

So, let us now get on with your life. What you are about to learn is as practical as balancing your bank account. Once you have learned these principles, you will be amazed at what you can really do and become.

Let us begin to open doors together. TODAY IS *YOUR* DAY.

– ObomBowen

INTRODUCTION

The field of psychology is a large area of social science that piques the interests of students at many colleges and universities throughout the United States. In fact, psychology is a top pursued major at a large number of schools. Students who want to delve into the vast subject matter in this field must start at the beginning – Psychology 101.

Introductory Psychology courses generally cover a similar curriculum of material including topics such as historical approaches to the field, how to employ the scientific method for use in psychological research, and a basic understanding of the major methods used in professional psychology.

There are a great many introductory psychology books available for instructors to choose from. Many of these publications are subsequent editions of an ongoing series of texts, indicating that those texts have maintained a high level of success over the years. In order to be included on this list, the introductory psychology textbook must be peer-reviewed, be used nationally, receive acclaim from both students and instructors, and have positive reviews online.

So why am I telling you all this? You might see this as useless and nothing to do with you and your growth, but the fact is you couldn't be more wrong. So let me just come out and say this right NOW – by the time you finish reading this book, you will have the equivalent to a MASTERS DEGREE level of understanding of not just psychology, but of human behavior and most importantly your behavior that's gotten you to this point in life. The reason you bought this book is because you wanted to change your life, consciously or unconsciously. Either way, you are in the right place because this book is going to teach you exactly how to do that.

First let me tell you that *Today Is the Day* is not just another "how to book" on success or changing your life. It is NOT about getting more money in your bank account – yet these secrets will help you to get exponentially MORE money than you've ever earned before.

It is NOT about increasing your wealth – yet these secrets will help you increase your wealth MORE than any course or book ever could.

Today Is the Day is THE ULTIMATE SHORTCUT.

So let's begin with me.

Growing up, I was the youngest of 12 brothers and 1 sister; being the youngest usually comes with making lots of mistakes. My family was a first-generation Guyanese family who came to the United States. While growing up with a very large family, I didn't really have a vast family network to guide me.

Rather, I had everyone and anyone I encountered who guided me. I learned everything on my own at first by being hard-headed; I made lots of mistakes. I am also a very independent person by nature, so I tend to listen to myself when it comes to direction. Sometimes this would lead to some bad decisions.

My mother and father were usually working to support us, so I was left many times to learn things on my own. My mother had me at an older age and, because I was her last, she had a great deal of experience in raising sons; I was the result of 11 other blueprints from the other siblings who came before me.

I grew up with a bad self-confidence problem and, to top that off, I had a pretty bad stuttering problem that made it even worse. I was also overweight. I was different in social situations because I was usually the only fat kid in my class and neighborhood, and this continued as I went off to the Marine Corps and into a professional career. Thank God for a strict physical fitness requirement standard in the Marines which enabled me to lose weight and begin a new life journey. (Later in Chapter 4 we will dive into this much deeper.)

One of the main factors that caused me to have self-confidence issues was the fact that I made many mistakes growing up, yet making those mistakes is the main reason for my self-discovery and foundation of the self-confidence I have today.

When I made mistakes and wrong choices, I would hear comments from others. Those comments usually told me things such as, I would never do well in school, I would never be able to do anything well, and so on and so forth. The problem, I have found, was that I began listening to those comments and would have the small talk in my mind before doing anything. I honestly didn't think I would ever be able to complete college, be good at public speaking, socialize with people, and the list goes on. (In Chapter 5 we will dive into this even deeper.)

The interesting thing is that I graduated at the top of my class with Suma Cum Laude distinction. I can also give a public speech without any problem and socialize with people in any situation. My chosen profession now is sales where I have to approach people I don't know, build a relationship, and sell the products. You would never guess a person with low self-confidence would ever be able to do this as their career, but I have done it successfully year after year.

So how did a stuttering fat kid with a severe self-confidence problem break out of his shell and overcome the "small negative self-talk" within his own mind to come out the other side the total opposite of what many had thought he would turn out to be? Well, in Chapters 9-12 you will learn it took years of not listening to the negativity that others gave, learning from my own experiences, and proving to myself that I am capable of anything. Know that you can do the same.

In this book, I will share some stories and exercises you can do right now that will enrich your life and give you a firm grasp and understanding for success. You will also learn how this all relates and how you can effectively change your life. But first, you may be asking, "Can this book really do that?"

The answer is YES!

With this in mind, the place to start is to see yourself living in abundance and you will attract it. The problem is that most people think about what they don't want, and it shows up over and over and over again. If you think about debt all the time, you're going to get more and more of it. Whether you're thinking about how bad it is or thinking about paying it off, that is what you will attract. In Chapter 9 pay particular attention because the main lesson will teach you this: the power of *my* imagination and *your* ability to use forethought allows you to project yourself into a new future – the future you want.

> **Every time someone has a thought, they are in the process of creation.**

The Law of Manifestation or the Power of the Subconscious Mind is always working, whether you understand and believe it or not. Every time someone has a thought, they are in the process of creation: something will manifest. You may choose to believe this or not, but it's all around us; all we have to do is open our eyes and look. The one who speaks most of illness has it. The one who speaks most about prosperity has it. The Law of Manifestation is evident everywhere around you. Quantum physics says that the mind is actually shaping the very thing that is being perceived.

There Are Two Things You Need to Be Aware of:

> 1. An affirmative thought is hundreds of times more powerful than a negative thought. This will help you to eliminate any degree of worry.

> 2. You are the mastermind of your own life, so you want to choose your thoughts carefully.

As we move forward, let's talk a little about success and how it works simply. First let's start with the Law of Manifestation which requires action. You will also learn that manifesting also comes from our thoughts; the topic is one which many of us do not wish to talk about. Action is the foundational key to all success.

It is best to know that without knowledge and a workable plan, you are gambling with little or no chance of success. Ronald Reagan once said, "The best minds are not in government; if any were, businesses would hire them away." I believe what he was trying to say was that if they knew it was possible, why not really do it and be the best minds?

The decisions that you make each day can actually catapult you to that next level of achievement. That next level is the value of time! Perhaps the best question you can memorize and repeat over and over is, "What is the most valuable use of my time right now?" Another question one should ask is, "Why even bother getting an education?" How do you convince anyone you are worth anything if you don't invest in yourself? Many of us are afraid to invest in ourselves, but fear melts when you take action towards a goal you really want.

There is a distinct difference between the wealthy and the poor. The wealthy plan for three generations, but poor people plan for Saturday night. It's always simple to take action, which is the antidote to despair. It is why one must always do things right. This will gratify some people and astonish the rest. We ask ourselves what or who is the best teacher. I've always said experience teaches us that it is much easier to prevent an enemy from positioning themselves than it is to dislodge them after they have gotten positioned.

Experience taught me a few things. One was to listen to your gut no matter how good something sounds on paper. The second was that you're generally better off sticking with what you know. And the third was that sometimes your best investments are the ones you don't make. First, you must have the courage to do or not do.

Wealthy people plan for three generations, but poor people plan for Saturday night.

Courage doesn't always roar. Sometimes courage is the quiet voice at the end of the day saying, "I will try again tomorrow." You must learn from the mistakes of others; you can't possibly live long enough to make them all yourself. If one can really master this, many of their coming years will be easier. In two days from now, tomorrow will be yesterday. So value each day and make it count. Know that if you view all the things that happen to you, both good and bad, as opportunities, then you operate on a higher level of consciousness.

The winners in life constantly think in terms of *I can, I will,* and *I am.* Losers, on the other hand, concentrate their waking thoughts on what they should have or would have done, or what they can't do. Albert Einstein once said, "Any intelligent fool can make things bigger, more complex.... It takes a touch of genius — and a lot of courage to move in the opposite direction."

I've come to understand that anyone can achieve their fullest potential.

Who we are might be predetermined, but the path we follow is always of our own choosing. Choose to be different, to be better. Choose to make a stand for you TODAY. Make *Today Is the Day* for you. We should never allow our fears or the expectations of others set the frontiers of our destiny. Your destiny can't be changed, but it can be challenged. Every man is born and every single man will die.

Martin Luther King, Jr. said to take the first step in faith. You don't have to see the whole staircase. Just take the first step. Take the first step with me now, and let's begin with a new working relationship for you.

Taking the first step in anything is always the most important, especially when it comes to success. Success is not the key to happiness. Happiness is the key to success. If you love what you are doing, you will be successful. With success, routine brings results. A disorganized genius is no match for the average person with a daily routine.

Time is important, but the quality of your life is directly determined by how you choose to spend your valuable time and with whom you choose to invest it. As we begin to move forward in this journey, don't forget to pack your courage for your journey to greatness. Learn to fly as fast as thought. In Chapters 13 and 14, much of this will be brought to life for you.

To be anywhere, you must first begin by knowing that you have already arrived. The goal comes first: we seek something we don't presently have (this is how the brain works). I always say if people throw rocks at you, collect them and build something. When someone tells me there is only one way to do things, it always lights a fire under my butt. My instant reaction is I'm going to prove them wrong.

Since becoming a Marine, whenever I made that statement I gained an even more determined will that drove me even harder.

If you can't excel with talent, triumph with effort. Today is the day. It's your effort that will make the new change. If you're interested in "balancing" work and pleasure, stop trying to balance them. Instead, make your work more pleasurable.

So with that, let us begin. Discipline is the bridge between goals and accomplishment. Accept responsibility for your life. Know that it is you who will get you where you want to go – no one else.

All my love, Obom

SECRET NUMBER ONE

Hidden in Plain Sight
— Understanding my blind spots and how they can limit my perception of the future.

Expand the Mind to Create the Future
— By setting out what is of value to me, I can expand my awareness of the resources available and learn that I am in control of my future.

How the Mind Works
— By understanding how my mind works, I can refine my decision-making process to create the life and future I want.

Beliefs Regulate Performance
— I regulate my behavior at the belief level, and I must change the picture of what is good enough for me in order to live and perform to my potential.

The Internal Conversation
— My beliefs are formed by the way I talk to myself. What others tell me won't become a part of me unless I give sanction, or agree, with it.

CHAPTER ONE

Hidden in Plain Sight

By understanding blind spots, you see how they can limit your perception of the future.

Overview

There is a logical and scientific method to look at the way human beings think. Because of our past histories and experiences we have had, our view of the world is limited. Unless we change the way we think, we will continue to live the lives we always have. This may be enough, but if we want more, then we must open our minds in order to see new possibilities. As Albert Einstein famously said, doing the same thing and expecting a different result is the very definition of insanity (Einstein).

Objectives

By the end of this chapter, you will understand:

- Scotomas and how they can limit me.
- By locking on to the way things have always been done, I'm blind to new possibilities.
- I need to be mindful of the "truths" that are given to me, as they may not be my truths.

Key Learning Principle

When my mind is fixed, I do not allow myself to live the life I'm capable of living. I want you to remember this as we go through this chapter. Our minds work just like a parachute – best when open.

Let me start off by telling you what this is all about. I think I'm going to break it into two parts. One is why you should change your mind. The second part, if I can convince you why you should change your mind, is how do you go about changing your mind? What value is it to you? What value is it going to be to your organization?

Now, what I'm going to explain to you isn't something that I've invented. This is scientifically based in the cognitive psychology field. My gift over the years, close to 20 years, is being able to explain it so clearly and so easily that you can apply it to yourself and cause your life and your organizational life to improve immensely.

All I'm going to do is speak to you in very logical and scientific terms on principles that are proven over years and are applied not only to an individual, but to any organization. If they are applied correctly, you will see enormous improvement in anything that you undertake. You have enormous potential lying asleep inside of you. How do you wake it up?

Well, that's what I'm about to tell you, but so many people are very hesitant about changing their mind. I'll talk to you about why there's a resistance to that also. I want you to know that it's okay to change your mind. I'll prove to you that it's okay to change your mind, and I'll prove to you that it's absolutely essential to change your mind.

Let me give you a fun test. I'm going to show you two teams of people. One dressed in white shirts, another dressed in black shirts. I want you to count the number of passes with a basketball made by the team dressed in white shirts only.

I'm going to ask you to look at a video I have on my YouTube Channel. For this to work 100% effectively, you have to follow the instructions directly, so don't read ahead. Reading ahead will only get you confused. Remember to count the number of passes made by the team dressed in white shirts only. Ready?

Go to Youtube.com/obombowen and type in "Today Is the Day Selective Attention Test."

Really, start watching the video and counting. Don't read any further until you watch. PROMISE?

Ok, good. Go to the link above.

DID you watch the video?

Okay, how many passes did you count? And where did *that* come from? Amazing though, isn't it? Isn't it amazing?

Let me explain to you a little bit more about why I said at first that it's important to change your mind. You let me make up your mind for you. You allowed me to instruct you. Of course, I was focusing you on something I thought. In this case, for me, I was making you feel what's important. Once I got you concentrating, focusing, and locking on to the team in white, your mind blocked out everything else in black. You didn't let yourself see anything but what I was instructing you or leading you to see.

The questions then are, "What else are you leaving out? Who has helped to shape your mind? Who is shaping your mind today? Who is telling you what you should look at, what you should do, what you could become, and how the world is constructed?"

This is the way we are. Once you make up your mind, "Ah, you've got it," boom, you build what is called a "scotoma," a blind spot to other options.

We cannot help ourselves. That is the way our minds work. So in your reality, in your comfort zones, what you see is that which is in your historical memory of the way your life is, the way the world is, the way your business is, you've already made up your mind. If there are other easier ways, better ways, new options, could it be, just like the gorilla, you can't see them? But then you are struggling hard to find new ways, and to change your life, and to make your life improve, and to make your life better.

You may come to the conclusion that, "There is no way. This is the only way. If there was another way, I'd perceive it, wouldn't I?" The answer, when you know how your mind works, is probably not. But if I can show you why you should change your mind, then what you'll find is that you'll see more options and opportunities. You'll see answers and solutions that you didn't see. It's almost like watching a magic show, a magician working on your scotomas. All of the sudden, they may make an elephant appear or a rabbit come out of a hat, and you say, "Wow."

Well, that's what I would like for you to know. You're going to be like a magician for the rest of your life. You're going to pull solutions out of the hat. You're going to find new opportunities. You're going to find new joy, new ways of running your life. It's not magical. It is knowing why you should change your mind and how to change your mind. When you find that out, life is better, easier, and faster. You'll love it.

The other thing you're going to need to learn is, "Well, then how do I go about doing this?" I will help you with that, so let's come back. What you just experienced, again, is a blind spot called a "scotoma." It is Greek for blindness. Scotomas can occur not only visually, but with sound. You can block out sound. You can block out taste, and smell, and feelings. All of your senses are blocking out information based upon what is important to you. The way your mind has been made up, the way you were raised, who your relationships are with, and who you listen to are forming the reality with which you guide your life.

When we know how our mind works and how to change our minds, then our dreams can get bigger. "I've got it" – then my dreams can get bigger. My life can be bigger. I can run my life. I can be that which I choose to be, and that's the gift I'm giving to you. The gift of knowing how your mind works and the processes to continually alter and change your mind closer to your true potential.

This works not only for one, but for your organizations because you talk to each other in your departments. You talk to each other in your social world. You talk to each other in your organizations, and you tell each other, "Watch the team in white. This is the way we run our day. This is the way we run our business," and when you give sanction, which means agree with that, you can't see the gorilla. But instead of the gorilla, you can't see opportunity, options, or resources.

When I first found this, I didn't see the gorilla either. But what went through my mind when I found out the cause is, "What else am I leaving out?" It's most likely not intelligence or aptitude. Most likely it's the way our minds are fixed, the way my mind is set that is not allowing me to live the life that I know I'm capable of living. That's my gift to you, so stay tuned. We've got a lot more to do.

This next section will be for you to take notes on your thoughts and answer some very *POWERFUL LIFE CHANGING QUESTIONS*:

Grow from Your Comfort-Zone

1. What are my beliefs about my life, business, work, or relationship as it is today?

_____

_____

_____

_____

_____

_____

_____

_____

_____

_____

_____

_____

_____

2. What do I believe because of what others have told me?

_____

_____

_____

_____

_____

_____

_____

_____

_____

_____

_____

_____

3. Where do I see potential in myself for greater growth?

_____
_____
_____
_____
_____
_____
_____
_____
_____
_____
_____
_____
_____
_____
_____

My Notes:

_____
_____
_____
_____
_____
_____
_____
_____
_____
_____
_____
_____
_____
_____
_____
_____
_____

_____

_____

_____

_____

_____

_____

_____

_____

So if you haven't as yet done so, do not go past this on to chapter two. I implore you to take an internal inventory now of where you are and work on changing or improving.

That starts with answering the questions and making notes about what came up for you while reading chapter one. If it's hard to accept where you are, there is still hope. You can change. That's exactly why you got this book. So make the change by starting NOW!

CHAPTER TWO

Expand the Mind to Create the Future

By setting out what is of value to me, I can expand my awareness of the resources available and learn that I am in control of my future.

Overview

The first thing we need to understand is that there is more to the world than our limited human senses can perceive. Because of the way we think, we don't "see" all there is to see about the possibilities of our businesses, our families, our relationships, and our lives. When we define what is of value to us, we begin to see the resources we need to move forward.

Objectives

By the end of this chapter, you will understand:

- I need to know what I am looking for.
- By setting out what is of value to me, I can expand my awareness of the resources available.
- I must take accountability for my own future.

Key Learning Principle

I am in control of my future. It is absolutely true that we can't change the past, but we can change our future. That concept is so important because we seem to dwell on the things that we cannot change, things that are long gone and forgotten.

What we picked up from the first chapter is that you're smarter than you thought and that there is opportunity that you cannot perceive. Well, let's take a look at that. I would like for you to stop being sensible. I would like for you to stop being quote, realistic. Now, let me frame that for you so it comes out better. Your senses are very limited. There is a reality throughout the universe or right in front of you that you cannot see.

But if you are traditionally the type of person that says, "I'm a realistic person, show me. I'm a sensible person, go ahead and show me. Can't show me, can you?" What you get into is a locked on, locked out mindset. You lock onto what is real for you or what is possible for you. When you do so, there may be opportunity, information, and resources available, but to you, you are stuck with the reality that you have caused in your own mind.

One more piece. Located at the base of your brain to the central cortex is a filter system called the reticular activating system. The reticular activating system is an actual net-like group of cells, again located from the base of your brain to the central cortex. The reticular activating system has the job of locking out, building a scotoma, a blind spot to information around you in your world that is not important to you.

The reticular activating system actually lets you read a book, watch a movie, and listen to a lecture. If the reticular activating system was not there, you could not concentrate or focus. You would be bombarded by too much information hitting your senses of sight, taste, smell, and feeling. You would be so distracted, you couldn't hear or see. The reticular activating system is an essential part of your ability to be high performance, but it screens out information. It just blocks out information without you knowing you're doing it.

You always think you're seeing the truth, so what the reticular activating system lets through to your central cortex of awareness is the only information you have decided is important to you. It lets two things get through. Value and Threat. Value. You decide what's important. Everything else is Scotoma out. That's why a mother can be sound asleep at night with a sleeping baby close by her while traffic goes by and airplanes fly overhead. The mother will sleep through these noises because they're not important to her. But if that baby awakens with the slightest cry in the middle of the night, the sound gets through her reticular activating system to her brain. Just like that the mother is awake.

It's not the decibel level that gets through; it's the value of the information that gets through. If the information is not of value, it doesn't get through. Sometimes you may say to yourself, I'm not smart at this. I'm not good at this. I can't get it through my thick head. I just can't seem to remember. It just doesn't come through.

Does it not come through because of your intelligence? Or does it not come through because it wasn't important to you? Have you ever read a book twice and nothing gets through? That's because you didn't know what you were looking for. You must know what you're looking for. Then the information gets through. Now if you will remember, the reason you need to change your mind is because you're going to determine in your future what is going to be important.

You're going to set goals out of your present comfort zone into your future reality, you're going to find information that you didn't know existed, and you're going to call yourself lucky. Otherwise, all you're letting get through your senses is information that was important to you yesterday, last year, or only at the present moment your world doesn't change much unless you change your mind. You're going to find later on that the goal comes first, and the goal has got to be out of your present reality. The goal needs to be something in your future, beyond your present comfort zone. Then you'll find it's amazing. You'll see information that leads you to the goal. It's like a person looking for a parking spot. If you can try this, set a goal in your mind as to where you want to park. As you drive down a very busy street, your subconscious is looking for clues because you programmed your mind with the desired future reality.

Your reticular activating system doesn't need to see a parking spot. It will see people approaching cars, and it will see heads in cars that are parked two blocks away. It will see exhaust, red lights flashing, and other clues. You are so smart, but you've got to let yourself and your mind seek something outside of your present reality. In doing so, you start gathering knowledge to lead you to your objective.

Some people say, "Well, that's just a coincidence." It could be, but it could also be the way your mind works. So, when you know why and how to change your mind, you must then set objectives and goals far beyond your present comfort zone. In doing so, all of the sudden, your world changes through your perception.

You decide to buy a new television set, a new car, or a new iPhone. As soon as you decided to buy it, you're going through your Facebook timeline or your local newspaper, when suddenly you see an ad for it. Well, if you went back and looked at past newspapers and newsfeeds, there would probably be an ad for that item, but you had a scotoma to it because you didn't need it.

No need, no get through. The goal comes first. This means you seek something that you don't presently have, visualize it in your mind, get it clear in your mind, and open your reticular activating system to conversations, ads in papers, and information. It seems to flood you. That's how your brain works.

You are smarter than you thought. You are more gifted than you know, but you must know why you should change your mind. If you don't change your mind, all you see is what is presently important to you. When you set a new importance, new information gets through. The goal comes first and then you perceive.

Oh, well if all this works, then why doesn't the father wake up when the baby cries? Doesn't he have a reticular activating system? Is it damaged? No! Now, you see the father has given up accountability. It's not in his department; it's not his job. It's not his job description, so your awareness shuts off if you give up accountability for your own goals. Why don't you find this for me? You must learn that if I am going to be a success, I've got to remain accountable, specific, and clear about what it is that I'm seeking or my reticular activating system doesn't work.

It only works on clarity, specificity, and accountability. If you don't change the reality with which you're presently living, all you see is what you saw yesterday. All you see is the reality of the way it was last year and say to yourself things don't change much. Life is about the same, but I want you to recognize that you are in control of your own future unless you choose to give up the control of your future. You must every day prepare yourself for your future. Prepare yourself for the goals you're seeking. Prepare yourself for what you intend to see. Otherwise, all you see is what you have prepared yourself for in the past. More to come about how your mind works. I believe you are starting to get it already.

This next section will be for you to take notes on your thoughts and answer the POWERFUL LIFE CHANGING QUESTIONS:

Grow from Your Comfort-Zone

1. List some examples where your RAS (Reticular Activating System) has led to what I needed:

_____
_____
_____
_____
_____
_____
_____
_____
_____
_____
_____
_____
_____
_____

2. Where in my life, business, or relationship could my RAS lead me to what I need?

_____
_____
_____
_____
_____
_____
_____
_____
_____
_____
_____
_____
_____

3. Where in my personal life have I given up accountability to another?

_____

_____

_____

_____

_____

_____

_____

_____

_____

_____

_____

_____

My Notes:

_____

_____

_____

_____

_____

_____

_____

_____

_____

_____

_____

_____

_____

_____

_____

If you haven't as yet done so, do not go on to the next chapter. I implore you to take an internal inventory now of where you are and work on changing or improving. That starts with answering the questions and making your notes about what came up for you while reading chapter two. If it's hard to accept where you are, there is always hope. You can change; that's exactly why you got this book. So, make the change by starting NOW!

If we accept that sooner rather than later, we would be one step closer to having true happiness and success. The past can sometimes be our adversary because we seem to let it take over and decide our futures. We cannot let the negativity of the past dictate our current lives and futures.

What I love the most about sharing the above information and tips is doing it live with an audience. From the stage, I watch the lightbulbs come on and see others know immediately that it's possible to have true love, success, or the ideal life. It is also amazing doing a radio interview and being able to interact with callers. With my readers, I'm always excited to get comments or questions on my Facebook page (FB.com/obombowen). Visit anytime and let me know how I can continually be of help or service to you.

I have an added an additional bonus for you. Here it is: you can go to my relationship website: www.globalfairytale.com to download and print a FREE copy of my actual affirmations to serve as a guide for you as you create your own. You will also find so much more on the BONUS tab. I wish you love and abundance. To that note in the next chapter, I can't wait to share with you more of the most powerful secrets that will transform and ignite the new you.

CHAPTER THREE

How the Mind Works

By understanding how my mind works, I can refine my decision-making process to create the life and future I want.

Overview

We discover that we are making decisions for our future, not based on what could be but on what has happened to us in the past. The purpose of memory is to help predict the future, but old patterns of behavior, like our habits and attitudes, can get in the way of moving forward. With a little examination, we can uncover old habits and attitudes that we can throw away and replace with new ones to help us create a new and exciting future.

Objectives

By the end of this chapter, you will understand:

- The four parts of the decision-making process: perception, association, evaluation, and making decisions.
- I need to watch for where my actions are taking me away from my goals, as there is probably an attitude getting in my way.
- That in order to move forward, I need to examine old habits that cause me to act with mindless efficiency.

Key Learning Principle

Keep the goal – just change the habits and attitudes. Remember, just as we all have limiting thought patterns, we all have limiting behaviors. Changing habits or behaviors requires that you make a list of the actions you want to change. Once you identify the problematic behaviors, only then can you really problem-solve and find new, supportive habits and behaviors to take their place.

Okay, what should be going through your mind is, "Wow, what else am I leaving out? Is there more?" Absolutely. Now, remember these two things. One, why do I need to change my mind? Two, how do I go about changing my mind? What is the benefit to me, my family, and the world around me? See, it's all in your mind. Now when I talk about the mind, I'm talking about how your brain works. It's just a way of explaining it, so I'm going to demonstrate here for you for a moment.

We will break our mind into three parts: the conscious, the subconscious, and the creative subconscious process. Now you don't really have parts like that, so don't look for them, but it's me being able to explain it more clearly, okay? The conscious part has four functions, one of which is perception for your senses. The second is association, the third is evaluation, and the fourth is decision making.

Your subconscious has two or three functions. One is to store reality; a second is to handle everything that is automatic. That will be your habits, attitudes, and reflex action. The creative subconscious process has four functions. One is to maintain reality or the status quo. The second is that it solves any problem or conflict that occurs. The third function is creating energy.

The fourth is teleological. Throughout this book, I'll be going through all of this. I'm just giving you a quick overview. Through perception, even before birth, you start gathering information about the world. All of your experiences, every book, every conversation, are stored somewhere in the neuron of your brain. Also stored is how you feel about it. It's stored in your limbic system. Your emotional history is also stored, so this reality is really your history. Inaccurate or accurate, doesn't matter. You call it the truth.

HOW THE MIND WORKS

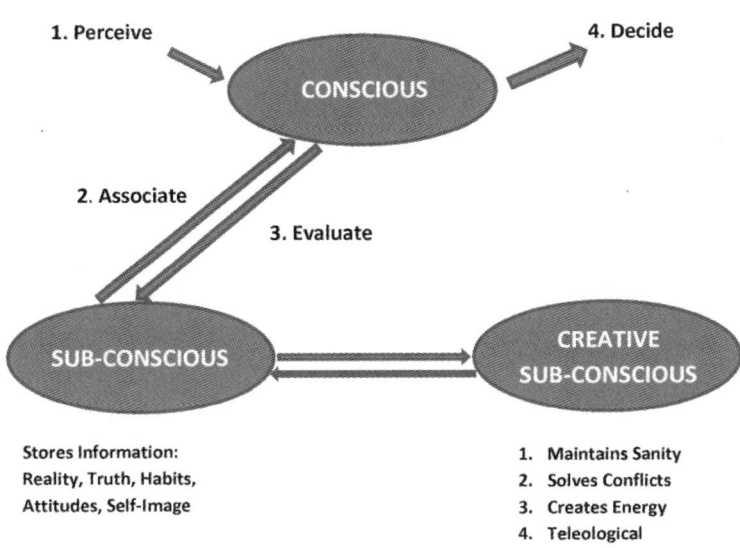

To you it is the truth, but you see you don't realize you're leaving the gorilla out or that this reality may not really be the truth. It is only that which you have stored from your history, your memory.

The problem is with all that reality you have stored about who you are, how you are, how good you are, and how much you can do. The creative subconscious process has one specific task of making sure you behave like the reality you know yourself to be or to make the world outside of you match the world inside of you.

When you say I've got to focus on the team in white, your mind doesn't let you see the black. Once you make up your mind saying "I'm stupid at this," even though you aren't, your subconscious must make you act stupid. Once you establish a reality in your mind, the creative subconscious isn't interested in helping you reach your potential. Its specific job is to maintain homeostasis. To maintain the reality that you have stored in your mind. To make you act and behave like you know you are. Is that accurate or did you leave something out?

Now the problem with this stored reality – as you approach today, tomorrow, or the next day – you perceive going to work, you perceive work, you perceive your relationships, you perceive the world around you, and you associate, which is the second function (the Sub-Conscious Mind). Have I seen anything like this before? So today you're not living in today; you are living, quite frankly, with your emotional history. Your reality of yesterday, so you balance what you are perceiving off of your stored reality.

The third function is evaluation (the Creative Sub-Conscious Mind). You then ask yourself, what is this probably leading me to? You are judging probabilities. Have I been by this before? Is it good? Is it not so good? Is it dangerous? Is it sweet? Is it sour? Is it hurtful? Is it painful? Is it harmful? You're judging always with your mind. Everything is being judged. That's the evaluation process. Then the fourth function is to decide, to do or not to do, to go or don't go, to buy or not buy.

Most of you are making your decisions not upon what can happen in your future. Most of you are making all of your decisions upon what has happened to you in your past. If you had a break up of a relationship that was very hurtful, that emotional history is stored inside of you. When you perceive getting involved with someone who seems to be a wonderful person, you also perceive and associate. You think to yourself, I seemed like this before? Uh-huh.

Your stored emotional history is then evoked and you ask yourself what is this probably leading me to? And you say more pain — so you decide not to get involved with a new person because of the old person. Most of you are making decisions in your life based upon your yesterday — not your today of what is possible.

With the processes, I'm going to teach you how you could change using affirmations and controlling your self-talk. With processes of visualization, you can change your emotional history. You can recreate a more accurate reality in which you will constantly be running your future. Otherwise it's like Norbert Wiener (the founding father of the computer) called the G.I.G.O. principle: "Garbage in, garbage out."

If you put misinformation into your computer, don't expect the right answers to come out. Or if you invested in some stock that didn't go well, you lost money. You perceive a new investment. You say to yourself, "Have I seen anything like this before?" what it's leading to and decide not to invest in the new one. This is done, not because of the new one, but because of what has happened to you in the past.

When you understand that you can change your mind with affirmations, visualization, and the control of your self-talk, you improve this history so that your life gets better. That's what I'm guiding you to and that's what I'm going to teach you. You must change your mind. I'll show you how to change your mind or your life stays the same or worse. Let's take another step now. Also stored in the subconscious are all of your attitudes. Your attitudes are stored emotional history, but the best definition of an attitude that I've ever seen comes from aeronautical technology.

(Pretend with me for a moment that you can see me extending my arms like an airplane.) If you would just look at my arms a moment like they would be the wings of an aircraft. Airplane pilots talk about the attitude of the airplane in the direction of which it is leaning and the relationship to a fixed point like the horizon. So an attitude very simply, if you can remember, is just the direction in which you are leaning. That's the simplest definition. The direction in which you are leaning.

If you lean towards something like some music, some food, relationships, or certain types of work, you're said to have a positive attitude. But if you perceive emotionally that something is going to be painful, hurtful, or embarrassing because of your emotional history, you subconsciously avoid it. When you perceive through your senses what this is leading you to and through your history, it says, you won't be embarrassed, you won't be made a fool of, and you won't lose face.

Most of us make decisions based on yesterday ... not on what is possible tomorrow.

What you have a tendency to do then is engage in subconscious creativity to remove yourself from that situation. You start procrastinating, creatively avoiding, creating scotomas, and creating obstacles that don't exist. Why? Because your emotional history says it will be painful, hurtful, or dangerous. Now that emotional history is called an attitude. That's stored here.

You need to change your mind and your emotional history, or your life will not get better. Many of you will start taking what is called time management courses to get yourself to do things you can't do. You don't need a time management course. You need to change your attitude. You don't need time management to do the things you love to do; you need time management to do the things you don't want to do.

So procrastination and creative avoidance occurs because you perceive some negative emotional situation occurring in your future. So you unconsciously procrastinate or stall. You engage in things that don't need to be done. You are full of attitudes that are blocking your future. You must change your mind, and part of your mind is that emotional history that is interfering with you releasing yourself to be the person you are capable of being.

Once I show you how to change your mind, you'll be able to change your attitudes. Otherwise, you'll set a goal but won't get yourself to do what's necessary. You'll then give up on the goal because you can't get yourself to do it. When you really need to just keep the goal and change your attitude. I'll show you how, and that's part of changing your mind. Now the last piece has to do with habits.

Remember when you were a child with your tongue stuck out while laboriously concentrating on tying your shoe? Remember how you kept repeating it over and over, until pretty soon you could do it without thinking? Riding a bicycle too. It was hard and difficult until you got it down. Playing the piano starts off on the conscious level. Then you repeat and repeat. Eventually you put it over to the subconscious. So in order to do anything really complex, it starts out as small bites or parts. Through repetition you turn it over to your subconscious, and you're in a state of flow.

That is true about your work. That is true about the way you run your life. You are a very efficient person and pride yourself on being efficient. You've got your day down well. You've got your work down well, and you're in a state of flow. The level of flow, your habitual flow, only gets you the results that you've gotten in the past. If you want to do more, be more, have more, you're going to need to change your habitual patterns. How do you do that? I'm going to teach you how.

Most of you are operating subconsciously in a state of mindless efficiency. Mindless efficiency. How you cook, what you do in the evenings, what you do socially, and what you do at work is a state of flow habitually. The problem is, if you don't change your mind, you're only going to get what that mindless efficiency will bring you and no more. By the way, when you're in a state of mindless efficiency, you subconsciously reject new information.

You subconsciously reject better ways; you subconsciously reject information that interferes with your mindless efficiency, so you've got to become mindfully efficient. You've got to be able to open your mind to new behavior, patterns, information, and ways of doing your work to take you to a new level of efficiency.

You must change your mind or don't expect things to happen any differently for you. You can temporarily change something, but you always go back to the dominant idea and the dominant ways that are stored in the neuron of your brain emotionally, habitually, and in your picture of who you are. It's all about changing your mind. Stay tuned. I'm going to teach you how.

In our Today Is The Day workshops, I vividly present the concepts and education in-person. I provide more of the revealing and productive insights into how you think and how your thoughts affect how you act. The tools and techniques we teach are easily recognizable stories and examples that can be applied immediately to help you reach your goals easily and enjoyably. Life is propelled out of the ordinary and into an exciting adventure. You can learn more about our workshops at: www.todayisthedaybook.com/workshops

Answer the Following POWERFUL LIFE CHANGING QUESTIONS:

Grow from Your Comfort-Zone

1. Where have I creatively avoided making a decision?

_____

_____

_____
_____
_____
_____
_____
_____
_____
_____
_____
_____
_____
_____

2. What negative habit or attitude lies beneath my avoidant behavior?

_____
_____
_____
_____
_____
_____
_____
_____
_____
_____
_____
_____
_____

3. What positive habit or attitude could I adopt that would help me make a good decision?

_____
_____
_____

_____
_____
_____
_____
_____
_____
_____
_____
_____
_____
_____

4. As I examine a typical day for me, what behaviors have I allowed to become habits? Are these helping me or hurting me?

_____
_____
_____
_____
_____
_____
_____
_____
_____
_____
_____
_____
_____
_____

My Notes:

_____
_____
_____

_____

_____

_____

_____

_____

_____

_____

_____

_____

_____

_____

_____

_____

_____

_____

_____

_____

_____

_____

So if you haven't done so, do not go past this onto chapter four. I implore you to take an internal inventory of where you are now and work on changing or improving. That starts with answering the questions and making your notes about what came up for you while reading chapter three. If it's hard to accept where you are, there is always hope. You can change; that's exactly why you got this book. RIGHT?

So make the change by starting NOW! When you attend one of our live Today Is the Day workshops, we go through each question in depth and I personally hold you accountable before moving on. So even though I'm not there with you personally, pretend I'm there now holding you accountable.

Take great comfort in knowing that ALL great feats are accomplished one small step at a time. TAKE THE SMALL STEPS!

They make a BIG difference. I would love to know how it worked for you; I enjoy the comments on my Facebook page (FB.com/obombowen), and I look forward to hearing from you soon. This is probably the simplest way I can help you remain accountable to your continued growth and success; if you're more like my wife and hands on, then join us at one of our upcoming workshops.

If you're ready to learn how to transform your Life, success, or marriage, join the next Today Is the Day workshop, the best life-transforming program. For more information, go to my website (www.todayisthedaybook.com). Give yourself this gift as a reward of investing in your happiness and growth. The greatest gift my wife and I have ever given ourselves was attending four growth and leadership and marriage retreats per year since 2010. We still do it to this day; you can never stop growing or investing in yourself.

CHAPTER FOUR

Beliefs Regulate Performance

I regulate my behavior at my belief level and must change the picture of what is good enough for me in order to live and perform to my potential.

Overview

That picture we hold in our subconscious – of ourselves, our families, our relationships, our organizations – gives us a standard at which we regulate our behavior. If we get too far above what is good enough for us or too far below what is good enough, we feel stressed. Our creative subconscious goes to work to bring us back to our standard, what is normal for us. In order to do more and be more, we need to change the picture of what is good enough for us.

Objectives

By the end of this chapter, you will understand:

- I regulate my behavior at my belief level.
- How to recognize when I'm above or below my standard of what is good enough for me.
- I must change the picture of what is good enough for me in order to live and perform to my potential.

Key Learning Principle

We self– regulate at the level of our beliefs, not at the level of our potential. Believe it or not, we talk to ourselves all the time. This conversation we have with ourselves is known as "self-talk" – it's the dialogue we have internally 24/7/365. In fact, self-talk provides the foundation of our beliefs, and these beliefs are played out every day in the words we use and in the behaviors we show to the world. Our self-talk is constantly building or reinforcing the beliefs we hold about ourselves and our ability to make things happen.

When adversity hits, stop if you can and listen to what you are saying, either out loud to colleagues or to yourself. Remember, your words out loud affect not just you, but those around you. The question really is this: What beliefs are you and your teams, partners, or children affirming with self-talk that may be holding you back from achieving new levels of performance?

True success is achieved when the mindset of individuals is aligned towards the same vision. By transforming your foundation of beliefs, habits, and attitudes, you will be ready to drive improvement in life, love, success, and relationship performance.

Hopefully, from our last chapter you could see that if you don't change your mind, you only allow yourself to perceive information that matches what your mind is prepared to see. In a large corporation, successful managers don't want to hear good ideas from people who they perceive as beneath them or younger than they are. "After all, I got the organization to where it is. It's running perfectly the way it should be running. It could not be better. If there was a better way, show me. Can't show me, can you?"

You can see the frustration of a younger generation who can see the gorilla, but they can't get the leadership to see it. You see the leadership isn't necessarily doing it intentionally, but the manager honest to goodness doesn't see. Does that make sense? You've got to feel accountable to help people see what you see. Don't just give up, but help them see the truth.

Let's go another step now. Let's start with something that keeps you stuck and keeps me stuck. This reality I have stored, the subconscious reality of the way my home looks, of whether I save money, or I don't save money. The reality I have about who I am and what I am. That reality or truth that is stored somehow keeps recreating itself in my world. See, once you know how you are, you don't need to wake up in the morning and remind yourself, "I'm forgetful." If you know you're forgetful, you subconsciously behave like the person you know yourself to be.

How does that happen? Life would be difficult if you knew you were forgetful, and you need to remember that you're forgetful. That would be hard. Once you know you're forgetful, it's all over. Your subconscious takes over and causes you to behave or act like the person you know yourself to be. Not only that, but you have in your mind an idea of the way your world looks, the way your apartment looks, the way your house looks, and the way your neighborhood looks. You have an idea in your mind about what kind of stores you let yourself go into and what kind of shows you like. It's all stored in the neurons of your brain.

The reality of where you belong is stored there, but that reality is very limiting. It's like a ceiling. It's like a lid on the use of your potential. Now I'm going to explain to you how this works. With this reality stored, your creative subconscious then is always observing in your mind, "How am I doing? Is what I'm behaving like the way my world is going? Is it the way it's supposed to be for me? Is this normal for me?"

When you perceive through your senses differences in your behavior, in the cleanliness of your home, or in the amount of money you have saved, something happens inside you. This system, the creative subconscious, has one special job; it has the job of solving the differences. It corrects for mistakes. It's correcting for mistakes subconsciously. Now, it's called homeostasis inside you. You're working for a balance of reality. You know that if you look at your bank account and see your bills far beneath what is normal for you, how are you going to feel? Not good, right?

You must act like the person you know yourself to be.

When you perceive your reality far beneath what is normal for you, you take corrective action. You work, save, and do what's essential to bring yourself back to your idea of the way things are supposed to be for you. If you can remember now, this image inside your mind, this picture recorded in the neurons of your brain is for you the way things are supposed to be. When you perceive your behavior, health, wealth, social life, or family beneath your standard in your mind of the way things are supposed to be, it stimulates creative action inside of you to correct for the mistake. To correct for the mistake, you say, "It's beneath me. This isn't good enough." You take corrective action.

What you need to know and what you're going to see later on because of this dynamic balance principle, is the self-correcting that goes on inside of you subconsciously. When you see yourself doing too good for you, you correct backward. If a marriage is going too well, you'll do something to disrupt it. If business is doing too well, you will do something to disrupt it. You self-regulate at what we call your comfort-zone of what is normal for you, the way things are supposed to be. You not only correct when things are beneath you, you correct when things are above you.

Teams who know they're supposed to lose when they're playing somebody but find themselves ahead in the contest ... are they happy? Yes, but do you know subconsciously they take corrective action to make mistakes to lose and then blame it on bad luck? Is it bad luck? Or is it that you corrected your idea of what is good enough for you? Or did you correct your idea of the way things are supposed to be for us? It is a reality of what is good enough. That is the level where you subconsciously check and balance your behavior and your action in order for you or your organization to really fulfill its potential. You've got to change your mind of what is good enough.

You've got to elevate your idea – and elevate your internal standards of the way things are supposed to be. This process will always work; it is the way human beings are. What you need to know is that, "If that is so, that's why I need to change my mind. Well, then how do I change my mind?"

That's what's coming in future chapters. It is essential that you change your mind or you'll keep sabotaging your own success. I know some of you love to play golf. You have in your mind what your total score is; you know how good you are. You could be on a wonderful course on a wonderful day. You then notice after a few holes, that you are doing too well, "My goodness, this is too good for me." Have you ever done that? "This is too good for me."

Your subconscious cells don't worry. What do you do on the next few holes? You do terrible; you do beneath you. That is the subconscious correction protecting you from acting stupid by doing things that are unlike you, it's called homeostasis. You must act like the person you know yourself to be. That's how your mind works. When you ask yourself to sustain performance personally or environmentally above your internal standard, stress occurs.

Whenever you're performing better than your normal, stress occurs in your human system. That stress triggers subconscious creative action to go back to being like yourself. When you're performing above your idea of what is normal for you, you are faking it. You are pretending you are that good. Your subconscious creates the stress, and you are relieved when you let go of your conscious effort and go back to being yourself. If you know how, you can change to a whole new level. You could do two times more. You can do three times more without stress, but not if you don't change your mind. Stress comes if you're beneath your idea of what's good enough or if you're above what's good enough.

Does this make sense to you? You can see it, can't you? If you see it in yourself, you can see it in others. You're limiting your potential, not because you don't have the potential, but because you have an accepted idea. You've accepted a reality of, "This is the way it is for me. This is the way it is in this business. This is the way it is in this country." These countries have a reality of what's good enough. A business has an idea of what is good enough, but you have potential far beyond it. Let's reach it, shall we? Stay tuned and I'll show you how.

Answer the following *POWERFUL LIFE CHANGING QUESTIONS* before going on to the next chapter:

Grow from Your Comfort-Zone

1. Where have I self-corrected for having "too much" for me? What did I do?

_____

_____

_____

_____

_____

_____
_____
_____
_____
_____
_____
_____
_____
_____
_____

2. Where have I self-corrected for having "too little" for me? What did I do?

_____
_____
_____
_____
_____
_____
_____
_____
_____
_____
_____
_____
_____
_____

3. As I examine the behavior of myself and my associates, where do I see opportunities to increase our idea of "good enough?"

_____
_____
_____
_____
_____
_____

_____
_____
_____
_____
_____
_____
_____
_____

My Notes:

_____
_____
_____
_____
_____
_____
_____
_____
_____
_____
_____
_____
_____
_____
_____
_____
_____
_____
_____
_____
_____

By now you should have already figured out what I'm going to say next... so, if you haven't as yet done so, do not go past this on to chapter five. I implore you to take an internal inventory of where you are now and work on changing or improving.

That starts with answering the questions and making your notes about what came up for you while reading chapter four. If it's hard to accept where you are, there is always hope. You can change. Yes, I do truly mean that. Think of it this way: you paid me to harp on you to do the work. Isn't that exactly why you got this book?

So make the change by starting NOW! Or you can attend one of our live Today Is the Day workshops. We go through each question in depth, and I personally hold you accountable before moving on. So even though I'm not there with you personally reading this LIVE, just pretend I'm there now holding you accountable. Fair enough?

In the next chapter, you'll be able to learn some key techniques that will burn an amazing change into your life. I can't wait to share them with you. And here's the best part: you're almost there. I hope for you, so far, that you gained and learned a lot.

I hope I was able to provide value to you. Join me on my page (FB.com/obombowen) and share your take away from chapter four. I look forward to being in touch. My main purpose for this book is not just to give you some great information and leave you alone. I want to connect and interact with you to bring this information more alive and have you bless not only your life but someone else's as well. With that said, let's dive into the next chapter.

Random thought and point: at the end of my public seminars, I'm always fascinated at the interaction between couples. "Honey, should we get The Today Is the Day Workshop or The Today Is the Day Retreat?" she asks.

"I don't care," he responds. "Get whatever you want."

I'm listening to this and thinking, "How could he miss this opportunity?" Not the opportunity to decide what to buy, but the opportunity to connect with her, to get involved with her. She didn't care what they bought. She didn't want an answer; she wanted company. She wanted his involvement, improvement, and life change together. If you are the other partner reading this, don't miss it again.

CHAPTER FIVE

The Internal Conversation

My beliefs are formed by the way I talk to myself. What others tell me won't become a part of me unless I give sanction, or agree, with it.

Overview

We talk to ourselves all the time. While we may not consciously be aware of this conversation, it is constantly building and reinforcing the beliefs we hold about ourselves.

It is the quality and quantity of these thoughts that is reproduced in the world outside us. If the business or life we have is not what we want, we need to take a look at that conversation we have with ourselves every moment of every day.

Objectives

By the end of this chapter, you will understand:

- That my beliefs are formed by the way I talk to myself.
- What others tell me will become a part of me, unless I give sanction, or agree, with it.
- Organizations, large or small, have their own self-talk, and it is reflected in outward performance.

Key Learning Principle

We build our own reality with our own thoughts. What does it sound like in your head? Sometimes I wish I could hop into someone's head and hear what they are really thinking.

Our thoughts are secret – and it's a good thing too. We are far more brutal in our minds than in reality. Here are the major questions I have for you: When you talk to yourself, are you nicer? Meaner? Harsher? Sweeter? Do your thoughts match your actions? Do you speak your mind?

Before we even dive into this chapter, make some notes regarding the previous questions:

My Notes:

_____

_____

_____

_____

_____

_____

_____

_____

_____

_____

_____

_____

_____

_____

_____

_____

_____

_____

_____

_____

_____

We're going to start getting into how to change your mind, including why you should change your mind. It has to do with how beliefs are formed. Again, let's just remind ourselves, you behave and act at your belief level. Not necessarily your potential level. Also, your beliefs affect your perception. Not only **how** you behave but **what** you allow yourself to hear or see. What and how? How particularly do beliefs get formed? Are you born with beliefs? Is it in your genes or is it second nature? Is it acquired?

Your beliefs, for the most part, I would say are acquired. You are not born with them. How do I acquire my beliefs? This is essential as you learn this discipline; this will change your life forever. Our beliefs are formed by the way we think. We as human beings think in three dimensions. The first dimension is we think with words.

The words create the second dimension, a picture. The third dimension is emotion, so it's words, pictures, and emotions. The three-dimensional form of thought, in the world of psycholinguistics, has a name that I want you to remember; it's called "self-talk." There's another word for this whole form of thinking. You'll hear me refer to it as an "affirmation."

An affirmation is a statement of fact; it's a statement of belief. When I say a statement of fact, it doesn't mean it's true. You can tell yourself things factually. Sometimes, it's only an opinion and has little to do with the truth. But the way your subconscious mind works, it doesn't reject what you tell it. It accepts what you tell it. It doesn't argue back, "That's not true. You are better than that." All it does is accept what you tell yourself and how you speak to yourself. Let's come back. You speak to yourself in three dimensions: words, pictures, and emotions.

Okay, so the words that we use give us the second dimension, but it's all about emotion also. You attach emotion, positive or negative, to every statement of fact, to every experience. You are constantly recording emotion in your limbic system. This three-dimensional form of thought is what builds the beliefs. As I'm speaking to you, you speak to yourself, let's say three times faster. When I stop speaking to you, you speed up an estimated six times faster. It is this conversation that's going on in your mind that is being recorded in the neurons of your brain. It is important to recognize that these thoughts you have don't disappear into the air like smoke. Every thought is being assimilated in the neurons of your brain. So with every thought, you are reinforcing or establishing a belief.

Every time that you remember or make a statement of fact with your self-talk, your subconscious accepts it. This reinforces the belief. Even if it's not true, it doesn't matter. With our own self-talk, we're describing to ourselves the world outside of us and how it operates.

We're telling ourselves how we feel about it, how we think about it, and we call that the truth. That's the reality of which we self-regulate our effectiveness. Everybody is building their own reality about work, about themselves personally, about them socially, and about anything. You're building your own reality with your own thoughts.

What if your thoughts are negative and destructive? What if your thoughts belittle you? What if your thoughts are degrading to yourself? What if your thoughts are hurtful thoughts? Then what kind of reality are you establishing into the neuron of your brain? What difference does that make? Here's the difference: once you get the belief established, you now behave like the person you know yourself to be.

You check and balance your behavior at your idea of who you are, at your idea of how good you are, and at your idea of the way things are. How did they get in there? You were telling you. Now, imagine yourself at three, two, or seven years old. You are with parents who are telling you that you are stupid, shameful, or not smart. They are handing you statements of fact to you; they are describing you as they see you.

In reality that doesn't become a part of your own mind until you agree with them. You must give sanction, which means agreement, to the statements coming from other people. Who was telling you who you were? Who was describing who you were? External people seeing you for you and describing you. You accepted the reality.

You build your own self-image with your own thoughts.

Now once you accept your own self-talk… that you are this way, you can't see the gorilla. You also can't see the keys to your car or your purse. You only let yourself perceive information that matches your identity, self-image, or what we call your personal self. That's all you're allowing to get through. Once I know I am this way, I only let myself behave this way. I only let myself perceive, and my world becomes very confining to the reality I have built with my own beliefs. Does that make sense? Isn't this amazing? It is amazing, isn't it?

So remember now we build our own self-image with our own thoughts. When you were a child growing up, you didn't know, so many of you are living with a history. In some cases of abuse by teachers, bosses, older brothers or sisters, or other people in your world, you were told how stupid, unwanted, or careless you were. Maybe you were even told where you belonged. You accept that often times because many of you were taught to respect authority. Somebody who was twelve when you were seven was an authority, and they were describing you for you.

Now you behave like you. Your self-talk is still going on. Most of you are going back in your history when you perceive something, and you're telling yourself that's like me, this is the way I am, I've always been that way, or this is who I am. With your present self-talk, you are repeating your history of who you were. You're reinforcing it and establishing it so solid that it's hard for you to go beyond your present description of who you are. You'll act in accordance with the truth as you presently believe it to be.

What is important is that you recognize you must control your self-talk or your self-talk will control you. One of the principles of your mind is you must change the self-talk that is going on. You may not be able to affect the external world around you, how people talk about you or how they're talking. But you can now — with your own discipline.

The discipline is how I control how I speak to myself, and I stop accepting the opinions around me like they are factual. Whether it's television, music, or whoever it might be. You must become skeptical of the information that is coming your way, because if you accept the wrong information you cannot see the gorilla. You cannot see the right information. If you accept the wrong reality, it affects how you behave, act, and work. It affects the world around you. It's more inside you than outside you. Does that make sense?

One time, my mentor and his wife were in London. Passing an open window, they overheard a woman yelling at her daughter, "Get away from me! I don't love you anymore! I don't want you around me, you're not my daughter!" The woman then walked across the street leaving the child by herself.

Suppose this happened only once, but you can see that the event is one that child will think about many times in her life. The events don't need to reoccur. All she needs to do is lay awake and remember what her mother said over and over. That's what builds your self-image.

It is not necessarily what was said that one time. It is that you repeat it with your own reiteration, your own memory. You go back and repeat these realities. You relive in your mind these histories of limiting, hurtful experiences. Make sense? You are recreating it in your world today. What you must learn to do in areas where your performance is far beneath what you want is take the approach I will teach you.

Change your self-talk. Visualize yourself, structure self-talk by changing the picture to the new level of effectiveness that you have the potential to be. Otherwise, your life will be as it was, today, tomorrow, and the next day. Unless something else happens, I must change the inside to change the outside.

You must eliminate all the questions like, "What's the matter with me anyway?" Have you ever made a mistake and asked yourself that question? It'll be all right if you stop there, but you go answer the question and keep answering it. Maybe for a year or longer, you've been asking yourself what's the matter with you. What you're doing is lowering your self-image with your negative self-talk. Your self-image and your effectiveness match. How could I have been so stupid? You ever do something like that, huh? You see it's all right if you ask the question, but what isn't all right is answering it. This is because in your mind, you are lowering your opinion and belief in yourself.

Would you think you behave at your belief level? Or do you believe at your actual potential level? You behave at your belief level. Your task is to eliminate all the sarcasm, devaluation, and belittlement. Eliminate all the self-defeating questions — what's the matter with me anyway? How could I be so stupid? It's got to be rejected by you. When people around you say it, they can say it. You just don't need to accept it.

If you have children, teach them to do the same. Make sense? When I learned this, it was revolutionary to me. This is how your mind is working. It's a discipline, and the most important discipline is knowing how to speak to yourself. Got it? Much more to come, so stay tuned.

Answer the following *LIFE CHANGING QUESTIONS* before going on to the next chapter:

Grow from Your Comfort-Zone

1. What is this self-talk in my family/relationship?

_____
_____
_____
_____
_____
_____
_____
_____
_____
_____
_____
_____
_____
_____

2. What is my self-talk like when work/business is good?

_____
_____
_____
_____
_____
_____
_____
_____
_____
_____
_____

_____
_____
_____
_____

3. What is my self-talk like when work/business is bad?

_____
_____
_____
_____
_____
_____
_____
_____
_____
_____
_____
_____
_____
_____

4. What are my organizations or relationship's self-talk like? How is this affecting our performance?

_____
_____
_____
_____
_____
_____
_____
_____
_____
_____
_____
_____

5. In what ways could I mentor my associates, or spouse, to improve our collective self-talk?

_____
_____
_____
_____
_____
_____
_____
_____
_____
_____
_____
_____
_____
_____

My Notes:

_____
_____
_____
_____
_____
_____
_____
_____
_____
_____
_____
_____
_____
_____

So if you haven't as yet done so, do not go past this on to chapter six. Take an internal inventory of where you are now in your internal conversation process and work on changing or improving by answering the questions and making your notes about what came up for you while reading chapter five.

Remember, there is always hope. You can change, which is the exact reason I believe you bought the Today Is the Day book, RIGHT? So make the changes by starting NOW! When you attend one of our live workshops, we go through each question in depth and I personally hold you accountable before moving on. So even though I'm not there reading with you personally, pretend I'm there now holding you accountable.

Take great comfort in knowing that ALL great feats are accomplished one small step at a time. TAKE THE SMALL STEPS!

They make a BIG difference. I would love to know how it worked for you; I enjoy the comments on my Facebook page (FB.com/obombowen), and I look forward to hearing from you soon.

This is probably the simplest way I can help you remain accountable to your continued growth and success. If you're more hands on like my wife, join us at one of our upcoming workshops. If you're ready to learn how to transform your life, success, or marriage, join the next Today Is the Day workshop, the best life-transforming program.

For more information, visit www.todayisthedaybook.com. Give yourself this gift as a reward of investing in your happiness and growth.

SECRET NUMBER TWO

Comfort Zones

— I have created my current comfort zones, most likely by neglect. Some of my current comfort zones are holding me back from expanding my life, work, and possibilities for my future.

The Next Time

— Learning why I need to give myself replacement pictures helps me determine my future. If I change what I think about, I can largely determine what happens to me.

Out of Order – Into Order

— Change offers me the opportunity to grow, but I must learn how to make my own opportunities. If I throw my system out of order, I can move to the new picture I have of my future.

Seeing Myself Into the Future

— The power of my imagination and my ability to use forethought allows me to project myself into a new future, the future I want.

Living in Today, Planning for Tomorrow

— Learn the discipline of seeing reality, yet holding the vision of what I want. All meaningful and lasting change begins on the inside.

CHAPTER SIX

Comfort Zones

I have created my current comfort zones, most likely by neglect. Some of my current comfort zones are holding me back from expanding my life, work, and possibilities for my future.

Overview

What have you gotten used to in your business, in your whole life, in your relationships? What do you believe is "normal" for you? In this chapter, we explore how we have arrived at this "normal," and what happens to us physically when we are thrown beyond the boundaries of what is "normal" for us. By understanding how we got these self-imposed boundaries, we are ready to learn how to expand into "new normals."

Objectives

By the end of this chapter, you will understand:

- How I have created my current comfort zones.
- Some comfort zones can keep me safe, and others can keep me from growing.
- Which of my current comfort zones are holding me back from expanding my life, my work, my business, and my relationships?

Key Learning Principle

As human beings, we seek the familiar. Many of us think of the "comfort zone" as a relic of '80s motivational psychology and a tagline on cheesy corporate "reach for success" posters. But in fact, the comfort zone is a useful psychological concept that can help you embrace risk and make changes in your life that can lead to real personal growth. In this chapter that's exactly what we are going to focus on.

Your comfort zone is a "behavioral space where your activities and behaviors fit a routine and pattern that minimizes stress and risk" – the operative words here being stress and risk. In our comfort zone, there is a sense of familiarity, security, and certainty. When we step outside of our comfort zone, we're taking a risk and opening ourselves up to the possibility of stress and anxiety; we're not quite sure what will happen and how we'll react.

Right now our self-image controls itself, regulates, restricts, and keeps you who you are. It applies to your culture. It applies to your business. It applies to your social life. Because of people, you talk to each other. You tell each .other the truth. You're describing to one another how the reality is. Then you all act out the reality according to the dominant reality.

Let's talk more about your comfort zone. Your self-image is like any regulating mechanism, like a wall thermostat that controls the temperature or climate in a room. If this was a thermostat, you would set the temperature to around 70 degrees. Now if the temperature rises above 70 degrees, an electrical impulse is sent to the cooling mechanism that turns it on and drops the temperature.

It's operating on electrical feedback. If it drops below 70 degrees, the electrical impulse would be sent to the heater to turn it on. Now you see, that would be very inefficient because it would be on and off repeatedly. In climate control, they leave a dead space of about two degrees on either side. The temperature needs to go to 72 before it activates the cooling agent or drop to 68 before it activates the heater.

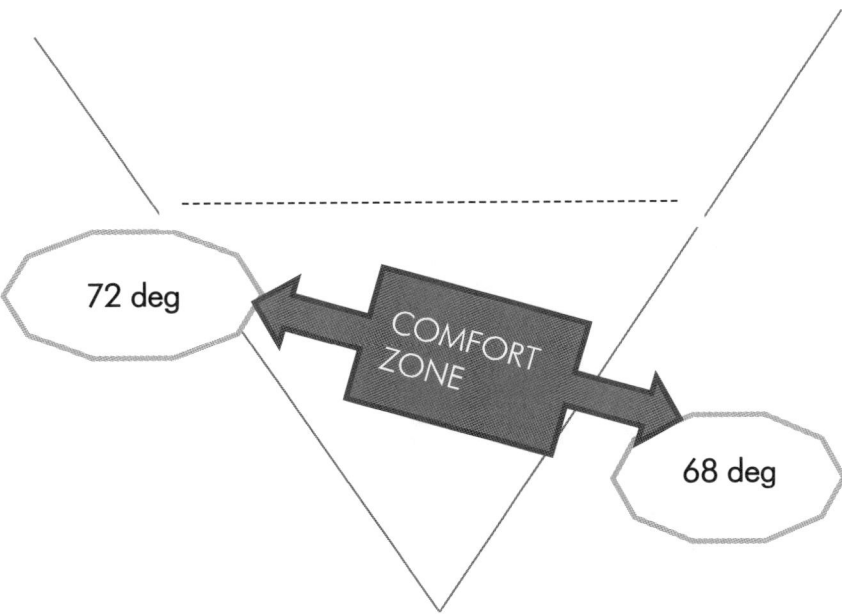

That dead space is referred to as a comfort zone. You can be comfortable within that temperature range, a comfort zone. What I wanted to do was give you a graphic illustration of how we behave and act. The open-ended graph is a representation of how much potential we have in any area of our life. The dotted line represents the ceiling, the lid, on the use of your potential.

This is established by your self-image. Your self-image is your dominant idea of how good you are. It's your dominant idea of who you are. It's your dominant idea of what is true. This self-image is your idea of what is normal for you. It is your idea of how things are for you. It is your dominant idea that most of you assimilated by neglect, not by intent.

You were assimilated by your parents, your teachers, by the reality with which you were brought up, the colors of people, and the languages. All of the familiar elements of your world that you have absorbed into the neurons of your brain become the reality with which you currently release your potential. You also don't need to behave morally exactly like yourself. You don't need to behave at work exactly like yourself.

You also allow yourself to behave reasonably close to the way you feel you are, not exactly like you perfectly. You also have a margin with which you allow yourself to free-flow inside, that's what we're going to call a comfort zone. When you perceive yourself with your behavior or your performance below your comfort zone, it isn't an electrical hit you get. It is an anxiety or tension feedback that you get.

When you observe your bank account falling beneath what you think it should be, you'll get upset about it. When you observe your performance athletically being beneath you, you get upset about it. When you see the friends you have are no longer suitable to you, you will get upset about it. Tension occurs when you perceive yourself beneath your idea of what is good enough.

That tension or that anxiety causes you to take action, subconsciously to go "back where I belong." It is important for you to recognize that this is a self-regulating effective mechanism inside you. When you see yourself being bigger or better than you or how you know yourself to be, tension and anxiety occur in your human system. It tells you subconsciously and creatively to go back where you belong, to go back to being yourself.

You self-regulate your effectiveness at your comfort zone where you're free of stress and tension – where it's normal for you, and where you can flow. What the problem is, your comfort zone becomes a prison that will not allow you to release your potential. It keeps you in jail. It keeps you confined. You don't know it's doing so. It's all subconscious. What you're going to see is that human beings fundamentally seek what is familiar to them. You seek what is familiar to you, colors of people, languages, environment, finances, etc.

We unconsciously seek the familiar. When you find yourself perceptually outside the familiar, you subconsciously create behavior inside yourself to go back to the way you're supposed to be. Got it? What you're going to see, it's all about changing your mind. You've got to change the level of who you are and what you expect to a higher level. You'll still have a comfort zone, but your comfort zone will be much above your present one.

You will always operate in that homeostasis or comfort zone self-regulating behavior but not at the level that you've accepted from some teacher, counselor, manager, boss, or family member. See, you're going to deliberately decide how you want to live. With the process of affirmation, the control of your self-talk, and the process of visualization, you're going to elevate your standards inside your own mind. Then you're going to do it again and again.

You will change your life by changing your mind. Now if we could just come back to what a comfort zone is, how it operates. When you find yourself outside of your comfort zone, environmentally or behaviorally, financially or socially, what you're saying to yourself is, "It's too good for me" or "It's not good enough for me." It is the differences that cause you to get uptight.

When you're out of your comfort zone, here's what happens. You become forgetful. You've prepared to give the interview. You know you're going to go into the interview for the promotion or for the new job. You know what you want to say, but when you go into that situation and feel out of place, your subconscious interferes with your memory. It's like you're watering the garden and suddenly someone comes up and kinks the hose behind you. Nothing comes out. Ever have somebody play that trick on you? Your memory is like that. It's squeezed off.

You forget what you were going to say. You could speak to a group while you're seated and talk to a friend, but if you're asked to talk to a thousand people on the same thing, your mind goes blank. You interfere with recall when you're out of your comfort zone. Your subconscious says, "Don't do it again. Don't put yourself in that situation."

You change your life by changing your mind.

Also, when you're out of your comfort zone, you block the input of information. When you're out of your comfort zone and people are giving you knowledge, information, or instructions, you can't get it out. You say, "I don't know. I'm just stupid. I just can't get it." Is it that you can't get it? Or is it that you're out of your comfort zone?

Most likely, you're just out of your comfort zone. When in fact, if you don't get it, you say to yourself, "I'm just dumb in that. I'm not good at that. I can't follow that, so I'll stay with the familiar. I'll go back to where I'm already good. I'll go back to where I've already come from. I'll go back to my old friends, my old job. I'll go back to my old world."

There's a way of getting out of that, but you've got to use your mind. You've got to create your future or otherwise you're going to repeat what you've always done, where you already feel good, where you already feel comfortable. The other thing that happens when you're out of your comfort zone, your muscles tighten up in your upper body. You get uptight, but your voice changes. So, other people know you're out of your comfort zone.

You ever get up to give a talk and sound funny? I must be getting laryngitis. It's not laryngitis. You're out of your comfort zone. Your upper body starts to tighten up, so the muscles in your upper body squeeze down on your rib cage and lungs. You say to yourself, "I've been under a lot of pressure lately." If you need fine motor skills, you become accident-prone. You make mistakes because it interferes athletically with your skills and abilities.

It isn't what you can do in practice. It's what can you do when you're actually playing the game. It's not what you can do when you're in your home. It's what you can do when you go away from home. It's not what you can do when you're familiar. Can you do it some place other than where you currently allow yourself to go? Yes, if you use visualization correctly. Yes, if you change your mind. No, if you don't change your mind. You'll blow it every time.

I've been under pressure. Your subconscious says, "Go back where you belong. Go back to the familiar. Go back. Don't make a fool of yourself. Stay with the familiar." The other thing that happens when you're out of your comfort zone, your stomach secretes more gastric juice than it needs. You'll say to yourself, "This can't be right. I've got a gut feeling about it. I've got an upset stomach. That always tells me what's right or wrong."

No, it just tells you you're out of place. It tells you you're trying to be better or worse than yourself. That's why you got it. Now you've got your stomach going now. You've got your rib cage caving down on your lungs. Your mind is blank. Your voice is changing. Your knees get shaky. You lose balance. The other thing that happens when you're out of your comfort zone, moisture appears on the surface of your skin whenever you don't tell the truth.

That's how the lie detector works. When you lie about who you are, where you are, or where you were, you immediately short the machine out. Moisture occurs. Your stomach is upset. Your rib cage is caving in on your lungs. Your voice is changing. You can't remember. You can't get anything out. What do you think you're going to tell yourself? Stay with the familiar. Don't go.

One other thing that occurs is that it stimulates creativity when you're out of your comfort zone. When you are incorrectly out of your comfort zone, you get negative creativity. Your mind gives you ideas of why you shouldn't go, why you shouldn't apply for the job, why you can't expand socially. It finds fault with the future that is unfamiliar. You find subconscious fault. You'll wake up with ten ideas of why you shouldn't go and why it wouldn't work. It's all in your mind, but to you it's real, but the truth is that it's not.

All you're doing is recreating your past into your future, unless you know the process of visualization, the affirmation process, the controlling of your self-talk. Once you do, you will let yourself travel fully out wherever you want to go, as long as you know the process. You will allow yourself to take yourself far beyond where you presently are. You can teach your children this. Those that are managing people, you can change. You can change. You can change, but not if you don't change your mind.

I love what Abraham Lincoln said, "Most people are about as happy as they make up their minds to be." Happy people realize happiness is a choice. They are not held hostage by their circumstances and do not seek happiness in people or possessions. They understand that when we stop chasing the world's definition of happiness, we begin to see that the decision to experience happiness has been right in front of us all along.

Research in the field of positive psychology continues to reinforce this understanding, that simply knowing that happiness is a choice and the same as you in your comfort zone. Fully experiencing it still requires a conscious decision to do so each day. How then might each of us begin to experience this joy? One way to start experiencing happiness and joy is through fostering trust going outside your comfort zone.

In closing this chapter, here is my spin on happiness and your comfort zone. My greatest lesson is that happiness is a choice not a result; it is a mental or emotional state of well-being, defined by positive or pleasant emotions ranging from contentment to intense joy. A variety of biological, psychological, religious, and philosophical approaches have striven to define happiness and identify its sources.

All I know is once I make up my mind to be happy, I'm happy. Once I make up my mind to live outside my comfort zone, I do. You will too.

Answer the following *LIFE CHANGING QUESTIONS* to get out of your comfort zone before going on to the next chapter:

Grow from Your Comfort-Zone

1. Some of my current comfort zone areas are:

_____

_____

_____

_____

_____

_____

_____

_____

_____

_____

_____

_____
_____
_____

2. Which ones are keeping me safe? Which ones are holding me back?

_____
_____
_____
_____
_____
_____
_____
_____
_____
_____
_____
_____
_____
_____

3. From these same lists, which comfort zone areas do I want to expand?

_____
_____
_____
_____
_____
_____
_____
_____
_____
_____
_____

_____
_____
_____

4. From my list of comfort zone areas I want to expand, what would my "new" comfort zones look like? How do I see them in my mind?

_____
_____
_____
_____
_____
_____
_____
_____
_____
_____
_____
_____
_____

My Notes:

_____
_____
_____
_____
_____
_____
_____
_____
_____

CHAPTER SEVEN

The Next Time

Learning why I need to give myself replacement pictures helps me determine my future. If I change what I think about, I can largely determine what happens to me.

Overview

Now that we have learned some of the root causes of what is holding us back from using our potential, we will learn how to perform and free-flow at our belief level with no conscious effort. As we understand this process, we will begin to learn how we can escalate our performance to a new level by giving ourselves the proper replacement pictures.

Objectives

By the end of this chapter, you will understand:

- Why I need to give myself replacement pictures to help me determine my future.
- If I change what I think about, I can largely determine what happens to me.
- There is a process to self-correct and focus on the future.
- How to coach and manage forward, rather than coaching backward

Key Learning Principle

We act like the persons we know ourselves to be. You may have heard it before, but it is such a strong statement: "We can only see things within others that we see within ourselves." I think this is one of the most challenging spiritual lessons we are here to learn. When I first read this statement in a spiritual book many years ago, it seemed very odd to me. Like most people, my first response was, "Surely, I do not act like a lot of people who annoy me and push my buttons." Interestingly, I find that when I facilitate spiritual classes, this statement typically elicits the same response from most others.

Everyone you meet is your mirror. Why is that?

We come to understand ourselves best through our relationships with other people. We can only be triggered by something we have experienced ourselves. The traits we tend to dislike in others are usually the traits we do not like about ourselves. We then tend to judge and criticize these characteristics. This calls to mind the analogy of pointing a blaming finger at someone. One finger is pointing at another person, and three are pointing back to us. In this chapter we will explore more of self-correcting.

When I found this information and started applying it, I was still active duty in the Marine Corps. I had never jumped out of an airplane until I was 23-years-old. My wife Ana and I do it all the time now. Until I was 23, I never really traveled to have fun or stayed in a hotel. We now travel all over the world every month.

When I served in the Marines, our income was so low I hardly had enough money at the end of the month to pay our bills. But that reality has changed immensely. Was it luck? No, I intentionally decided to use that which I'm teaching to change the inside of me. There's much more than that. I studied more, I developed myself, and I took myself far beyond where I would allow myself to go.

As I changed my mind, I had a passion for knowledge. I read and studied. I've got to have more knowledge in order to be able to fulfill what it is I'm creating in my mind. I didn't even know I was in a comfort zone. I just wouldn't let myself go into certain stores that were too good for me. I wouldn't let myself go into restaurants that were too good for me. I always looked at people that were really wealthy and rich and say, "I could never be like that." See, my comfort zone was so small because the rest of the Marines I was serving with were all about the same. So I could see people that were far beyond that, but oh no, that's not us. We don't belong there.

Everyone you meet is your mirror.

But with this knowledge, I recognized the causality of that and fixed it. Now, how do we get there? Let's come back and review a little bit more. So as you were being raised, most of us without intent just assimilated day after day what our neighborhood was like. What did your father do? What does your friend's father do for a living? What are you going to be when you grow up? What are the opportunities? Well, you see it only through the reality of the people around you.

Then you have counselors or teachers, who are telling you, perhaps with aptitude tests, where you belong in the future and what you can do. You come up with dreams bigger than theirs, or bigger than your grandparents, or bigger than your own parents, and they start scolding you. Let's be realistic. Let's be sensible. Why don't you get back where you belong? You'll only be disappointed when you start thinking things like that.

Some of you, because of the color of your skin, if you were raised in a prejudiced country, were restricted even though you had potential. So, some of those rules and realities were and are quite real. Religious prejudice, racial prejudice, economic prejudice, and so on. You fell for it, stuck it in your mind, and cooperated. Sometimes to save your own lives, of course.

The important thing here is, you are probably under-living your life. Not because you intentionally did, but you're not growing because you're not intentionally changing it either.

I want you to be very careful about people around you who are describing you for you. Who do you allow to tell you whether you are beautiful or not? Who do you allow to tell you whether you are capable or smart or not? When you go back in your history, people who were describing you in high school or work that had their own small comfort zones were intimidated every time you started thinking bigger than them. You have allowed people outside of you to describe you. You didn't know any better. You resisted for a few, but then you accepted what they told you.

Remember — words trigger what? Pictures, you record pictures. The emotion that's attached to it all becomes a part of your reality. Remember, it doesn't just happen that one time. It's actually occurring every time you think about it. You reiterate it with your own self-talk.

Coaches film your practices. They record your games. Then, for those who have been in sports, what do they do to the team? After the game, they sit you down and show you everything. What you've done wrong. They show it over and over and over until you get it down. They're coaching backward. If we record or visualize what's wrong with us, we repeat the emotional or pictorial memory each time we go on to the field.

You must see that there's a right way to correct people. It isn't that you let them make mistakes. As you're going to see later on, the right way to correct people without sticking them in the old reality, is to stop the behavior and give them a replacement picture. It's all about the replacement pictures.

You're operating on a picture that is beneath you. You're operating on a reality formed in the neuron of your brain, your social world, behavior, work, and finances. Then you keep re-creating it. What you must do is replace the picture to be the one that you expected your behavior to be like in the future. It's all about a different picture.

If you're a coach that has a player named Paul not performing correctly, you would say, "Stop it, Paul." Being positive doesn't mean you're permissive. That's where people make a big mistake. It means you don't tell them what to do wrong. What you would say if Paul made a mistake is, "Stop it. You're too good for that. You're better than that."

Now that's not enough. He needs a picture to replace the one that he isn't operating on. You need to tell Paul what to do right. It's all about the replacement pictures. You, as a leader or manager, will stop your behavior, but you're not going to say, "Why did you do that? Tell me. Why were you so stupid?"

Or you say to your spouse, "I don't know why you're doing that. Haven't I told you a hundred times what you're doing wrong? How many more times do I need to tell you before I get it through your thick head? A few more, I guess. It hasn't worked so far." You see, the more I tell you what's wrong with you, the more you record what's wrong with you and the more you behave like what is wrong with you.

If you have a child that leaves their clothes on the floor, what do you tell the child? "You're always leaving your clothes all over the floor." The kid says, "I know. I'm good at it." You've been telling me I've been leaving my clothes on the floor forever, now I've got to behave like me, or go crazy, so I act like the person I know myself to be. Often times you have described others the way you see them historically, not as they can be.

Good coaches, leaders, and mentors, you must stop telling yourselves how bad you've been, in the present moment. All you'll do is repeat it. In order to change, you must change your mind about how good you are, who you are. A good mentor saw more in you than you are presently behaving like or presently doing. They saw in their imagination, you in the future. Then they described you in the future, as though you actually were that person. If you could go back and remember, it would probably sound like, "I see you as being ..."

You respond, "huh, me? Me?" So what they were doing is describing not what you have been. They're describing you not even as you've ever done but as you have the potential to become.

Now the way they were doing it was first person present tense. It's something we're going to learn. It is not that you're going to be; it is that you are. Right now, in my mind. You can see that gets into Gestalt psychology. It is dynamic balance. It is throwing your system out of order by helping you envision a future better than you're presently living. When you see yourself out of order, you're going to grow into order. Out of order into order. But if you keep describing the child or the behavior of the person that you go to, or yourself as you presently see it, then tomorrow looks like today.

The key is seeing yourself into the future as you can be before you are, and that's the way you're going to describe yourself. That's the way you're going to lead people. That's the way you're going to talk to yourself from now on.

Let's talk ourselves into the future. Do you see how that works? This is the way you're going to talk to yourself. Stop telling yourself you're dumb. Stop telling yourself you're forgetful. Stop telling yourself the reality that you don't want because all you'll do is re-create it. What you must do is see yourself in the future, as you choose to be, and talk to yourself like that. What you must say to yourself when you observe your behavior (I'll give you this later on) is, "No more of that. I'm better than that." The next time tell yourself what you will do differently. See, there are four levels of self-talk.

The lowest level is negative resonation. No way, can't be done, I'm stupid, it's over, it's ... negative resonation.

The second level, you'll hear people say,

> I should.
> I could.
> I wish.

You know, I should lose weight. I could lose weight, I ought to lose weight, I just won't.

It's recognizing a problem with no intention of fixing it.

I should save money, I could save money, I ought to save money, I'm just not going to.

So whenever you hear should, could, would, if only, and I wish, you'll not see a change in yourself or anybody else.

Now, the third level is like a vow.

No more,
No more, I quit.
No more, it's over.
Stop. No more. It's a vow.

But you're teleological. You seek images, you seek pictures. When you tell yourself, no more, what are you going to do?

What are you going to do? Well, you are more likely to go back to your old ways because you have not yet set the correct replacement picture.

The fourth level is all about the next time. You tell yourself the image that you are seeking. You talk to yourself about the image that you are seeking.

It's all about the replacement picture.

Socially.
Economically,
Behaviorally, how you want your tomorrow to be,
It's all about the future. But it's the future as though it actually exists.

So stop listening to external people talk you backward. Reject what they have to say if it doesn't fit who you are becoming. Who's creating your reality? From now on, you are. Stay tuned, we have a lot more to do.

Your key to the Four Levels of Self-Talk

1. Negative Resignation
2. Recognition of the Problem
3. Vow – "No More"
4. Replacement Picture

Answer the following *LIFE CHANGING QUESTIONS* to get you out of your comfort zone before going on to the next chapter:

Grow from Your Comfort-Zone

1. If I move toward what I think about, what do I want for my future?

_____

_____

_____

_____

_____

_____

_____

_____

_____

_____

_____

_____

_____

2. Based on what I want, what adjustments do I need to make to my self-talk and self-image in order to be successful?

_____

_____

_____

_____

_____

_____

_____

_____

_____

_____

_____

_____

_____

3. What self-talk statements have I used or use now to reinforce my behavior in regard to my family/job/career/relationship? List examples.

_____

_____

_____

_____

_____

_____

_____

_____

_____

_____

_____

_____

_____

My Notes:

_____

_____

_____

_____

_____

_____

_____

_____

_____

_____

_____

_____

_____

_____

_____

CHAPTER EIGHT

Out of Order – Into Order

Change offers me the opportunity to grow, but I must learn how to make my own opportunities. If I throw my system out of order, I can move to the new picture I have of my future.

Overview

We have been learning that in order to grow, we must change the way we think. As we go deeper into how the human mind works, we discover that our energy and creativity come from having a problem to solve. By giving ourselves new levels to obtain, we are giving ourselves problems to solve and energizing our lives.

Objectives

By the end of this chapter, you will understand:

- Three of the four functions of the creative subconscious: maintain sanity, solve or resolve conflict, and create energy or drive to solve problems.
- Gestalt psychology and how my mind is constantly working for order.
- Why it is necessary to throw my system out of order, in order to grow.

- Why the new picture must be dominant in order for change to take place.

Key Learning Principle

Human beings are always working for order in their minds. Neuroscience confirms that to be truly happy, you will always need something more. What's the sign of a life well lived? If you were to judge by LinkedIn resumes alone, you might be impressed by prestigious job titles and accolades. But in person, the importance of these formal achievements quickly fade.

Whether we're striving for a new job, more meaningful relationships, or personal enlightenment, we need to actively want something more in order to live well. In fact, neuroscience shows that the act of seeking itself, rather than the goals we realize, is key to satisfaction.

Neuroscientist Jaak Panskepp argues that of the seven core instincts in the human brain (anger, fear, panic-grief, maternal care, pleasure/lust, play, and seeking), seeking is the most important. All mammals have this seeking system, says Panskepp, wherein dopamine, a neurotransmitter linked to reward and pleasure, is also involved in coordinating planning activities.

This means animals are rewarded for exploring their surroundings and seeking new information for survival. It can also explain why, if rats are given access to a lever that causes them to receive an electric shock, they will repeatedly electrocute themselves.

However, the human desire to seek can help make sense of studies showing that achieving major goals, or even winning the lottery, doesn't cause long-term changes in happiness. But our drive to look ahead needn't cause a permanent state of dissatisfaction, as seeking is itself a fulfilling activity. In this chapter we're going to talk more about how to change your mind. I think you're finding out why you should change your mind.

You're stuck in your comfort zone, and it affects your perception. It becomes a prison of restriction if you don't learn how to stretch your mind. Or the old way was to just make yourself do it, force yourself to do it, which is not a healthy way. It's a matter of changing your mind and letting yourself do it. Now what we need to know is a little bit more about how the mind works. Let me review for you but add one more step.

You may remember that we talked about the conscious, the subconscious, and the creative subconscious process. I also talked about the creative subconscious having four functions. One was to maintain sanity or reality, the status quo. The second was to solve or resolve conflicts. That's where we are right now.

We have created an image of reality on the subconscious level. It is your idea of the way the world is, my life is, and the way people are. It is my present reality or my present comfort zone. Now, whenever I perceive information outside of me that is different than the information that I have in my subconscious, that's called a problem or conflict. A conflict is when something doesn't taste right, look right, smell right, or feel right to you.

"That doesn't sound right to me." Okay? Now keep in mind, this statement was to me meaning you. I don't know if you've ever walked into your home, an office building, or some other place and the picture or painting on the wall was crooked. Does it bother you? Okay. It drives you crazy because you know how it's supposed to be in your mind. Your perception of sight is telling you, "Hey, it's crooked."

It's not congruent with the wall. It's not the way it's supposed to be. When this happens, your perceived reality through your senses is the information you are bouncing off your idea of what is stored in your historical memory of the way business is supposed to be, the way people are supposed to be, the way my children are supposed to be to you, and even the way the world is supposed to be. And when it isn't that way, it disturbs you. Got it?

The simplest definition of Gestalt is human beings are always working for order in their mind. That the outside needs to match the inside idea, like the picture on the wall. Whenever you perceive an incompletion or an incongruence, something that isn't matching my mind the way it's supposed to be, you call that a problem.

A problem to you or a problem to me could be different, but a problem simply is when the situation in my mind doesn't match the reality that I'm perceiving. Whenever that happens I feel out of order in my mind. Now according to the Gestalt psychology, human beings are always working to have order in their mind. We want the outside to match the inside so we feel free of stress, anxiety,

Human beings are always working for order in their minds.

and tension. When it doesn't match, we have anxiety and tension. Follow? So it seems you're always working inside your head to get rid of the anxiety and tension.

If I was born with my fingers stuck together, that's the way it's supposed to be. Every morning that I wake up and they're still stuck together, I'm going to feel okay. If I wake up one morning and my fingers are apart, it doesn't look right to me. That's not the way it's always been. It's not the way it's supposed to be.

My mind is telling me, I've got a problem. The way a human mind is constructed, we have to solve the problem. So when we perceive disorder, we create energy inside of our human system to restore order, to put it back together. Once it's together, I don't need any energy, so my energy shuts off.

So what am I telling you? You get energy which is motivation when you have a problem. No problem, no energy. Goal setting, you're going to see, is changing the status quo, throwing your system out of order to deliberately motivate yourself with energy to succeed and achieve. You want to be out of order if you're going to seek and be your best. The other thing that you know, we need more than just energy to put things together, we need ideas.

There's another word for ideas called creativity. I need some ideas. If your fingers aren't together as they're supposed to be, your subconscious creatively doesn't need to give you an idea. You don't need ideas. See, it isn't going to just overwhelm you with ideas that you don't need, but when you are out of order, you get creative. Ideas come when you perceive disorder not when you perceive order.

You're going to see that goal-setting and changing is a matter throwing your human system or your organizational system out of order. Then you get energy. Then you get ideas to put back to order. Got it? You want to learn to deliberately cause a problem for yourself. Sounds silly, but it's not. It's not a bad problem to have. It's a problem to improve your life. It's a problem to improve your income, the way your home looks, or the way your car is.

It's creating a problem to improve your environment, your community, or your society. See you can't sit and wait for good ideas and then set the goal, but if you set it correctly, you will get ideas. You will learn that you don't need to know how before you set the goal.

By setting correctly, you will invent the how. When you're out of order, as an example, one of my hands is the old way, the way you've always been, the way business is, the way your house looks, the way your family is, or the way your bank account is, this is just the truth as it "is" or you know it to be.

My other hand is the desired way, the new way, the vision; this is the ideal way I would like to have. This is what I would like to be. When you begin to visualize the new way, and you realize the old way doesn't look like the new way, you create internal incongruences, and that results in what's called a problem.

Now, energy is going to be released. Creativity is going to be released. But here is the key: your mind doesn't care in which direction you use your creativity. It doesn't care if you go back to your old way, and it doesn't care if you go to the new way.

You need to know what determines the direction your mind will use creativity or energy? What determines the direction? The strongest picture will determine the direction, if that strongest picture is of the old comfort zone and old image – of the way you've always been; or this is the way we are in this business, or this is the way this department is and your goal is something new.

If the old way is more dominant then all of your energy is used to take that idea and return it back to the status quo. You take your creativity and find reasons why the timing isn't right, it's a stupid idea, we shouldn't be there, or we've got to go back.

Your strongest picture will move you.

You get ideas to go back to your old friends, your old income, or your old way. But if the new way is made dominant in your mind, then the new comfort zone outside of your present comfort zone will harness the creativity and ideas. You invent the way to your goal. You don't even need to know how to do it. What you need is to make what you are seeking so vivid in your mind it's as though it actually exists.

You will learn to do that with visualizations, with using your imagination which is called forethought. I'll show you how to write your goals correctly and how to use your affirmation process to strengthen your goal. You've got to have a process to make the future that you're seeking more dominant than the one you're presently living in. What you'll see is that as you visualize the new and do it strongly, you become dissatisfied with where you are.

There's no growth without creating dissatisfaction in yourself. If in fact the goals you're seeking aren't your goals but they're being imposed upon you by the management or by the company, you will not use your energy. If you as a manager or leader are imposing your goals on another person, then it has to be your energy and your creativity.

The people around you in the workforce are trying to keep the picture straight on the wall. You as the leader are coming and tipping the picture. Everybody that works there says, "Hey, that doesn't look right." Then they put it right back the way they believe it's supposed to be.

It's all in your mind. You must change your mind or stay in the status quo. It's all about changing your mind. Now, it isn't a bad thing. It's a good thing. That's how we progress. That's how commercials work on television. They get you to envision driving a new car. Then you drive the new car and find fault with your old car. Does that make sense? It works with husbands too. You start visualizing a better one. You find fault with the one you've got, and he's always been that bad. It isn't like he all of a sudden got bad.

Imagine you want to build a kitchen. Have you ever started thinking about a new kitchen in your mind? Then you cook in the kitchen and before long refuse to cook in the unsanitary stinking mess of a kitchen, but it was all right two months ago. How'd it get bad in two months? See what happens? You're changing your mind. The way the world is supposed to be and the world you're living in doesn't match, so you correct it in the direction of the strongest picture. More to come.

Answer the following *LIFE CHANGING QUESTIONS* to get you out of your comfort zone before going on to the next chapter:

Grow from Your Comfort-Zone

1. How do I feel when I see a picture on the wall hanging crooked? Does it bother me? What do I do?

_____
_____
_____
_____
_____
_____
_____
_____
_____
_____
_____
_____
_____
_____

2. Where do we have a "crooked picture" in our organization/relationship/life/business?

_____
_____
_____
_____
_____
_____

_____
_____
_____
_____
_____
_____
_____
_____

3. Am I fixing the picture by moving it back to "the way it always has been" or am I moving to a new reality?

_____
_____
_____
_____
_____
_____
_____
_____
_____
_____
_____
_____
_____

My Notes:

_____
_____
_____
_____
_____
_____

_____

_____

_____

So if you haven't as yet done so, do not go past this chapter on to the next chapter. Take an internal inventory of where you are now in your internal conversation process. Work on changing or improving by answering the questions and making your notes about what came up for you while reading chapter eight.

Remember, there is always hope. You can change, which is the exact reason I believe you bought the Today Is the Day BOOK, RIGHT? So make the changes by starting NOW! When you attend one of our live workshops, we go through each question in depth, and I personally hold you accountable before moving on. So even though I'm not there reading with you personally, pretend I'm there now holding you accountable.

Take great comfort in knowing that all feats are accomplished one small step at a time. TAKE THE SMALL STEPS!

They make a BIG difference. I would love to know how it's working for you; I enjoy the comments on my Facebook page (FB.com/obombowen), and I look forward to hearing from you soon. This is probably the simplest way I can help you remain accountable to your continued growth and success.

If you're more like my wife and prefer a hands-on experience, then join us at one of our upcoming workshops. If you're ready to learn how to transform your life, success, or marriage, join the next Today Is the Day workshop, the best life-transforming program. For more information, go to my website (www.todayisthedaybook.com). Give yourself this gift as a reward of investing in your happiness and growth.

CHAPTER NINE

Seeing Myself into the Future

The power of my imagination and my ability to use forethought allows me to project myself into a new future – the future I want.

Overview

As we begin to create those dominant pictures of what we want for our futures, we gather the tools that will allow us to see ourselves operating in the future with ease. By using our imaginations and forethought, we create that magnetic draw to our desired future.

Objectives

By the end of this chapter, you will understand:

- The power of my imagination and my ability to use forethought to project myself into a new future.
- The importance of using first person, present tense, experiential imagery.
- The value in throwing myself and my organization out of order, to create a new order.

Key Learning Principle

We act in accordance with the truth as we believe it to be. How much control do you believe you have over what happens to you in life? In this chapter, let's talk about how our feelings about who is in control affect end-results.

Some people believe they have very little control over what happens to them. When good things occur, they believe it's mostly a matter of luck or circumstance. They don't set goals or plan very far ahead because they think that how things turn out is beyond their control.

Their tension and stress levels are generally very high, as you might expect, and they often feel overwhelmed, helpless, and hopeless. Strangely enough, when bad things happen, instead of blaming circumstances or luck, they tend to blame themselves.

The bad news is that how much control we believe we have over our lives is generally a direct result of the way we were treated when we were very young. The good news is that this condition, which has been called "learned helplessness," doesn't have to be permanent.

You can learn to take charge of your life and look at things differently. The fact is that when your attitude changes, the results you get also change. Yes, that is a fact, not just my opinion. The research is there to back it up. Your attitude is learned. And the results you get depend as much – or more – on your attitude, as anything else.

If you're interested in putting an end to feeling like a victim, congratulations on picking up this book, *Today Is the Day*, as a start. Or get involved in our reputable personal growth program. Attend one of our live workshops. You can register at www.TodayistheDaybook.com … what are you waiting for? Why not do it today?

Let's go back now to how our mind works. If you remember, I said that the events that occur in your life are not what is happening in your head. It is you observing light reflecting off of objects and you describing to yourself what you think is taking place. Some of us even tell ourselves what we think the other person is thinking and call that the truth. There is a formula about how reality is created, and I'm giving you this formula because this is necessary for you to change your mind about your new comfort zone and future.

Your imagination is also called forethought. Forethought, thinking forward. Thinking forward with your imagination. You can anticipate what the weekend will look like. You can anticipate what you want for dinner. You can anticipate the way you'd like to decorate your home. You can anticipate what you want for a career. You can anticipate the one you would like for a life partner. You can anticipate with your mind. Using your forethought to project into the future of an end that does not yet exist.

Also, you use your imagination to create the reality that you presently have. It isn't what actually happened, it's the reality that you imagined was happening that is recorded. Try to remember this formula: $I \times V = R$. We'll come back and use this again. The "I" stands for Imagination. V stands for Vividness. By vividness, we mean any time we get a clear picture with emotions. When we have the picture repeated, it becomes R, our reality on the subconscious level.

Remember the little girl in London from my example? If it happened one time, her version is still what is being created in her mind. That evening, unable to sleep, she probably reiterated the event. She maybe even enhanced it clearly in her mind, reliving it with emotion.

She's had it repeated only in her imagination, but it became her reality because she did it over and over and over. The realities you have stored are the realities both positive and/or negative, but it is your imagination that has created the reality. Then you act and behave like it's true. You act in accordance with the truth as you have come to believe it to be.

When you were a child, did you believe in ghosts? Did you believe in monsters? Did you behave like they were there, but it was in your imagination? See? Your reality is still being created the same way. What you're going to learn using this formula is instead of going backward, we're going to go forward. Instead of recalling what has happened, although we will use what is useful from the past, we're going to create the future of ourselves actually participating at a higher level of performance, at the next level of performance. We are going to see ourselves in situations that frightened us. With our imaginations, we'll reconstruct emotional histories that will be suitable for us as adults.

We act in accordance with the truth as we believe it to be.

We are going to recreate our future with the same formula. You will learn to write your goals out. You'll learn to visualize your future the way you are more capable, more positive in response, at a higher level of effectiveness. You're going to reestablish a reality in your mind, the same way you have established the one that presently exists. This isn't something that I've invented.

It is the way your present reality has been created, and we're going to use that to envision us at a higher level of performance. Responding appropriately emotionally, allowing ourselves to go far beyond what our present comfort zones will allow us, but we're going to do it safely in our mind.

We take ourselves into the future, but the way you must take yourself is in the first person present tense. It doesn't do you any good to see someone else performing, to see someone else being wealthy, to see someone else being a great athlete. It does not change your mind.

My mentor was once having a lunch with one of his son-in-laws at a restaurant in West Seattle where he lived. He said, "Look at that man across the street." Here was a derelict, a person getting into a garbage can looking for scraps. "Do you think if you keep watching him that you will become a bum or a derelict?"

His son-in-law kept looking, but he didn't say anything. After a short while, he said, "I could never see myself living like that."

My mentor said, "That's my point. You don't change by observing another. Only if you see yourself personally into the garbage can will it change the construct of your mind."

See, it's first person present tense experiential imagery that changes the neuron of your brain as though it's actually happening to you. Watching somebody else be wealthy won't make you wealthy. I said to him, "If this all worked that way, I would take you to where Bill Gates lives. I would put you all in front of his house and have you watch Bill Gates until you became wealthy, but I know what you'd say, 'I can't see myself living like Bill Gates.'"

That proves my point. You must see yourself that way, because as you see yourself, that changes your inner image. It throws your comfort zone, your new level, out of order, and you seek the order. You've got to see yourself at that level of performance. You must see yourself into that future, not someone else. That's how your mind works. That's how the formula works.

It isn't just a matter of looking at your neighbor. It isn't a matter of looking at somebody who is really wonderful. You're going to see yourself as wonderful, not someone else. I don't know if you've ever been someplace and seen somebody give a presentation or do something wonderful and say, "I really admire that person."

Have you done that? Like you really admire that person. What I'm going to show you is you must go from admiration to assimilation. Most people just stay in the state of admiration. "I admire that person and how they work. I admire that person and their family. I admire the way she looks. I admire what they have." You see that doesn't change the construct of your brain at all.

You must see yourself having that job, car, wealth, trait, or personality. It's first person present tense, experiential imagery, a clear picture. But it's got to be present tense imagery. It's got to be first person imagery. It's got to be experiential imagery, or your reality or comfort zone stays the same.

You've got to practice yourself at another level. Practice yourself going and being someone who you know you're capable of being. You take yourself in your imagination to the next plateau. You take yourself in your imagination with the right emotion into the next situation that you choose to travel, that you choose to move to.

That's what a good mentor did. Remember they always saw more in you than you saw in yourself. The way they described you had you travel in your mind into the future.

A good mentor said, "I see you, _____ (insert your name in the blank), as being. I see you, _____, as being. I don't mean someday. I mean right now in my mind I see you."

They guided your imagination into that vision into that job. Then you saw where you were. But you saw where they thought you were, and you've got a problem. You start studying, you start developing, you start, "Gosh, I can't stay still. I've got to go. I've got to go."

See, now you'll either become dependent on your manager or somebody outside of you creating who you will be when you grow up or learn to do it yourself. I learned to do it myself. Twenty-seven years ago, I started seeing myself at a level far beyond where I was, far beyond my comfort zone, far beyond my status quo.

I would set the aspiration of the goal and grow into it. When I first started doing it, doubling my income seemed like it was almost impossible. As a Marine in those days, it was about $750 a month. To double my income was $1,500. I could see other people making that kind of money, but I couldn't see anybody like me or even myself making that money.

I didn't know how to do it, but as I changed my mind I grew into who I needed to be in order to leave the Marine Corps. In that case, as the Marine Corps locked me in 4 years at a time, and I had to take my classroom out into the world. I had to change my idea of what being successful and serving my country was, and then I learned how to sell. I needed to be a better entrepreneur and gather more information. I didn't have a lot of things I knew I needed, but I wouldn't have lacked any of it if I stayed in my comfort zone. I would have set goals only within my comfort zone.

Maybe you are doing the same.

Some of your goals – maybe becoming a chief executive officer in the next six months – might be completely unrealistic, but within that framework, there are steps that you can take. But you've got to think outside of that framework, past that, even for the value of your organization.

Stop thinking about how things are and being frozen in that reality. Start looking at what can we be, what can we do? That's exactly what I started doing, and then I wanted to double my income again! I'm a genius inside — and so are you. You'll find the way if you do it.

That's how your mind works, but this is the formula. The formula created your reality and it is the one that still creates your reality. Remember the three dimensions of self-talk: words, pictures, and emotions. That's what this is. You're going to talk yourself into your future.

Answer the following *LIFE CHANGING QUESTIONS* to get you out of your comfort zone before going on to the next chapter:

Grow from Your Comfort-Zone

1. What do I need to do to see myself in my goals experientially?

_____
_____
_____
_____
_____
_____
_____
_____
_____
_____
_____
_____
_____
_____
_____
_____

2. Who has been a meaningful mentor in my life? What difference did it make?

_____

_____

_____

_____

_____

_____

_____

_____

_____

_____

_____

_____

_____

_____

3. How can I use this knowledge about imagination, forethought, and experiential imagery to help myself and others in my organization to set bigger goals?

_____

_____

_____

_____

_____

_____

_____

_____

_____

_____

_____

_____

_____

_____

My Notes:

_____

_____

_____

_____

_____

_____

_____

_____

_____

_____

_____

_____

_____

_____

_____

_____

_____

_____

_____

_____

So if you haven't as yet done so, do not go past this chapter on to chapter ten. Take an internal inventory of where you are now in your internal conversation process. Work on changing or improving by answering the questions and making your notes about what came up for you while reading chapter nine.

Remember, there is always hope. You can change, which is the exact reason I believe you bought the Today Is the Day BOOK, RIGHT? So make the changes by starting NOW! When you attend one of our live workshops, we go through each question in-depth and I personally hold you accountable before moving on. So even though I'm not there personally reading with you, pretend I'm there now holding you accountable.

Take great comfort in knowing that ALL great feats are accomplished one small step at a time. So please – TAKE THE SMALL STEPS! They make a BIG difference.

I would love to know how it's working for you. I enjoy the comments on my Facebook page (FB.com/obombowen), and I look forward to hearing from you soon. This is probably the simplest way I can help you remain accountable to your continued growth and success.

If you're more like my wife and prefer a hands-on experience, then join us at one of our upcoming workshops. If you're ready to learn how to transform your life, success, or marriage, join the next Today Is the Day workshop, the best life-transforming program. For more information, go to my website (www.todayisthedaybook.com). Give yourself this gift as a reward of investing in your happiness and growth.

CHAPTER TEN

Living in Today, Planning for Tomorrow

Learn the discipline of seeing reality and yet holding the vision of what I want. All meaningful and lasting change begins on the inside.

Overview

The challenge of change is seeing reality as it is today while holding the vision for what we want. This discrepancy is what causes our energy and creativity to emerge. We want to make certain that what we want is the dominant image we hold, so that we move to a more powerful future.

Objectives

By the end of this chapter, you will understand:

- My thoughts cause my dominant images and I am drawn toward them.
- The discipline of seeing reality, and yet holding the vision of what I want.
- All meaningful and lasting change begins on the inside.
- I cannot impose lasting change, on myself or anyone else, from the outside.

Key Learning Principle

We move toward and become like what we think about. Our present thoughts determine our future.

That is because: "Thinking Makes It So."

Here are some things that don't exist: A bad day, a boring book, a demeaning job, and an ugly dress.

Why do I say that? Shakespeare had this idea in mind when he said, "Nothing is good or bad, but thinking makes it so." You see, if the dress was truly ugly, every single person we asked would say, "Yes, that is ugly."

But what are the chances of that happening? And if the day was truly bad, then no one could possibly be having a good day on that date, could they? And even if two people share the very same experience on the same day, one of them may call it bad and the other one may say, "Now wait a minute. There is another way to look at it."

And that is exactly my point. There is always another way of looking at things, so why in the world would you voluntarily choose a way that is negative, devaluing, or makes you feel badly? You have the ability to control your thoughts and emotions. The first step is believing that not only is it possible, but it is possible for you. And when you feel you can do it, you then try. And the more you try, the better you get at it.

Negative feelings that once dominated you can be made to go away, and the time it takes you to banish them will grow shorter and shorter. Until one day you may surprise yourself by saying, "Golly, I cannot remember the last time I really felt angry or depressed!" I know you can do it!

You know we think in pictures, and by now you should know one more piece that you move toward. Because you're teleological, you seek objects; you move toward that which your mind dwells on. It's very important that you understand, your present thoughts determine your future. You move toward and you become like that which you consistently think about. If you think in pictures, which we do, then when you get an idea, vision, or thought in your mind, you're unconsciously drawn to that.

Important to know is that you're drawn to the thought whether it's going to be helpful or good for you, or not helpful or no good for you. Doesn't matter. Do you know anybody that worries? Worrying is thinking about what you don't want to have happen. You're drawn toward it and trying to get away from it, so you move toward that which you think about.

Your present thoughts determine your future. They determine your mood tomorrow or what's going to happen this evening. Once you set your own mood, you set the stage for your reality. You break Scotomas with your present thoughts, or you create Scotomas with your present thoughts.

If you move toward and become like that which you think about and your present thoughts determine your future, you can understand a child learning to ride a bicycle. They are not very good. They are coming down a path and see a big rock in front of them, but they don't want to hit it. They don't know any better, and they just keep looking at the rock they don't want to hit. They don't even realize that their physiology or the way they steer their bicycle is attached to what they're looking at, so they keep looking at what they don't want to hit and smacko! Right into the rock. Then they get mad at the rock.

Now think about it, you do the same thing when you're driving a car. Consciously or unconsciously, you are looking where you want your car to go. You're steering, adjusting the brake and speed. It's all subconscious. It's connected to what you're looking at. Formula One race car drivers are taught that if your car is going out of control and heading to the wall, you don't want to look at the wall. If you look at the wall, you'll unconsciously turn your car into what you don't want to hit. Got it? So what are they taught? They are taught to look to the recovery point. What should the child learn about the rock? Look where you want to go when you have a problem. That could be a devastating problem with your business. It could be a problem with your relationship. It could be a problem with your health.

If you have a problem, it's all right to see the problem. But the next thing you must do is think about what you do want instead of what you don't want. You don't ignore the problem, but once you see the situation then you've got to ask yourself, "What will it look like when I don't have the problem? What will it look like when it's fixed?" If you're hanging around, socializing, or working with people who are always complaining about what's wrong, they're saying, "I'm a realist. I'm telling you what's wrong. You're talking about pie-in-the-sky, future stuff. I'm talking about real stuff." They stick right where they are.

Did you ever know anybody that was accident prone? What do you suppose accident prone people think about? Having accidents! If you care about an accident-prone person, before they leave the house you might tell them, "Be careful, dear. You know how you are." "Oh, I almost forgot." "I'm glad you didn't forget. It's because I love you. I need to keep reminding you of your problem." The more you dwell on your problem, the more likely you will recreate it. You move toward it and become like that which you think about. Your present thoughts determine your future.

It's discipline to control your present thoughts, your present self-talk. You can get trapped around people who are gloom and doom and, "Isn't it awful?" You can get trapped around people who are talking about what isn't right instead of what is right. If they are dominant in your culture, they're leading your whole culture, social group, or business into that which we don't want to have happen. They think they're great prophets. "See? I told you the bad was going to happen, and it did."

There are three time frames most people live in. If you live in the past and sit around talking about how things used to be, then you are causing yourself to go backward and wonder why things don't change. It could happen accidentally. If the best of your life was behind you and you keep dwelling on how things used to be, the good old days, then the future is very bleak. Not much happens. In fact, you become discontent with where you are and want to go back to the good old days.

Astronauts who have gone to the moon and back get trapped in history. If your child saw them in a supermarket, they'd want their autograph because of what they have done, not what they're going to do. You get trapped in the past, and not much progress takes place because you move towards what you think about. You become like that which you think about.

If you're trapped in the present moment and the way things are, people around you are saying, "This is the way it is," then tomorrow looks like today. You just keep rolling it over one day after the other because you move toward what you think about. You think in pictures. You're drawn to the picture, and the picture is stuck, then you're stuck. What's it like where you're working? What is the dominant conversation when you get together with your family?

There's a right time to think about the past and present, but if you're going to move yourself or your organization forward, then you want to think about the future as though it already exists, it's the future in the present tense. You project forward. You see the game already won. You see the building built. You see the degree as mine, I've got it. The sale is made, the situation is done. You see it in your mind. Now, you look at the way things are normally and what happens is you come back and say,

"Hey, we haven't even started to build the building. I haven't even started school yet. We haven't even made the presentation." I know. You have a problem. But you're supposed to.

As a leader, speak of the future as though it exists, like a good mentor would. Remember, they see you as they saw you in their mind as though you already were. That's what causes the Gestalt. That's what releases the energy and the creativity. It's not enough to say, "Someday I will be nice. Someday I will be wealthy. Someday I'm going to be... "

> **Stop dwelling on where you don't want to be ... dwell on where you want to be.**

"Someday" does not have drive. My energy is not released. Remember, I've got to throw my system out of order, and that causes the energy and the ideas. Seeing the future already created, getting a dose of reality, is like, "My gosh! It's not, but I say that I am. Wow, I have a problem." You're supposed to have a problem. Do you see how your mind works?

Those three time frames are very important. Where do you spend your time? What do you do with your time? What are your social conversations like? What's it like when you socialize? What's it like in your business? What's it going to be like?

If you had cancer or were sick, do you wait until you're well to think well? Or should you think well and take yourself out of the present state into the desired state? This is no different in your business, marriage, or life. Stop dwelling on where you don't want to be. Dwell on where you do want to be. Hold the picture. If you're going to lock onto something, lock onto the picture of the future the way you want it. Take the present and move it into the future. That is how your mind works.

When you start writing your goals (which I'm going to teach you), you will write them as though you already possess them. You'll write your goals as though you've already accomplished them. You will feel the emotion of having already successfully accomplished what you are seeking. You are going to automatically focus yourself on a better future, the new desired state.

One more now. I alluded to this earlier, but this is an important piece that all meaningful and lasting change must come from the inside. All meaningful change and lasting change starts on the inside, in your imagination, and works its way out into reality.

I'm going to add one more piece to this. You cannot impose change from the outside that's lasting or meaningful. I can't force you to change. You can't force another person to change. You can't impose your will without having some form of muscle or some form of intimidation or some form of forcing a person, but the moment you let go of the force, they will always go back to the way it was.

I see sometimes dumb things happening where the leader of a country thinks, "We can force our will on another country, and we'll get them to change as long as we keep the power and the guns on top of them."

Remove that and they will go back to their dominant idea of who they are. You always return to your dominant idea of who you are. You cannot impose change from the outside. All meaningful and lasting change starts here, and works its way out. That is what you're going to learn how to do. Does that make sense?

Answer the following *LIFE CHANGING & THOUGHT PROVOKING QUESTIONS* to get you out of your comfort zone before going on to the next chapter and the final secret:

Grow From Your Comfort-Zone

1. What challenge or problem is most in need of a solution right now for me personally? Organizationally? Relationally?

_____

_____

_____

_____

_____

_____

_____

_____

_____

_____

_____

_____

_____

_____

_____

_____

_____

2. How can I help others in my family, organization, or relationship see the vision for the future and be drawn to it?

_____

_____

_____

_____

_____

_____

_____

_____

_____

———————————————————
———————————————————
———————————————————
———————————————————
———————————————————
———————————————————

3. How can I help others see beyond the rock in the road?

———————————————————
———————————————————
———————————————————
———————————————————
———————————————————
———————————————————
———————————————————
———————————————————
———————————————————
———————————————————
———————————————————
———————————————————
———————————————————

My Notes:

———————————————————
———————————————————
———————————————————
———————————————————
———————————————————
———————————————————
———————————————————
———————————————————

So if you haven't as yet done so, do not go past this chapter on to chapter eleven. Take an internal inventory of where you are now in your internal conversation process. Work on changing or improving by answering the questions and making your notes about what came up for you while reading chapter ten.

Remember, there is always hope. You can change, which is the exact reason I believe you bought the Today Is the Day BOOK, RIGHT? So make the changes by starting NOW! When you attend one of our live workshops, we go through each question in depth and I personally hold you accountable before moving on. So even though I'm not there personally reading with you, pretend I'm there now holding you accountable.

Take great comfort in knowing that ALL great feats are accomplished one small step at a time. TAKE THE SMALL STEPS! They make a BIG difference. I would love to know how it's working for you. I enjoy the comments on my Facebook page (FB.com/obombowen), and I look forward to hearing from you soon. This is probably the simplest way I can help you remain accountable to your continued growth and success.

If you're more like my wife and prefer a hands-on experience, then join us at one of our upcoming workshops. If you're ready to learn how to transform your life, success, or marriage, join the next Today Is the Day workshop, the best life-transforming program. For more information, go to my website (www.todayisthedaybook.com). Give yourself this gift as a reward of investing in your happiness and growth.

Secret Number Three

The Tools for Change
— Learn the tools and processes that lead to sustainable growth and change in every aspect of life.

It's My Choice
— Motivation can be negative and restrictive, which causes me to push back or be constructive. Putting my life on a "want-to" basis moves me forward, beyond my present limitations.

Yes, I Am Good!
— It is time for me to take charge of my estimation of my worth and stop relying on the opinion of others.

Goal-Setting Through
— In order to keep from flattening out, I need to reset my goals as I approach their accomplishment, which keeps me constantly moving forward.

Successful and Significant
— Yesterday's dreams are today's necessities. Today's dreams are tomorrow's opportunities!

CHAPTER ELEVEN

The Tools for Change

Learn the tools and processes that lead to sustainable growth and change in every aspect of life.

Overview

All that we have learned so far has been preparation for learning the tools and skills that we can use to achieve our goals for a lifetime. With the knowledge we have about how the mind works and how we can identify those beliefs and attitudes that have held us back in the past, we can now employ the principles and guidelines to create and sustain positive growth and change in our lives and in our work.

Objectives

By the end of this chapter, you will understand:

- That affirmations are simply my goals put into a format that creates replacement pictures in my mind.
- The eleven guidelines for writing effective affirmations.
- How effectively written affirmations can create a magnetic draw to the future I want.
- The process of visualizing my affirmations – by reading, picturing, and feeling the emotions – to unleash the power and creativity of my mind.

Key Learning Principle

As you visualize the new, you become dissatisfied with the old.

What makes people want to change? Notice, I didn't say "think they should change." Let's talk about the answer.

There are many things that make people think they should change, and all of them add up to pressure from outside themselves. It may be disapproval from a family member or friend. It may be social or cultural norms. It may be fear of punishment or humiliation.

But when the pressure to change is coming from the outside world, our desire to change is probably going to disappear as soon as the pressure is removed. The results of our change efforts are not very likely to last. What makes people really want to change is pressure coming from inside. Most important is the desire to move toward greater experiences of pleasure.

Next comes the knowledge that if we don't change, we will be violating our own standards, failing to live like the person we know ourselves to be. It also helps if we realize that the results of not changing will be far more painful than any discomfort we may create for ourselves if we do change. A technique that's really useful when it comes to creating positive and lasting change is to use the power of your imagination.

You can create vivid mental pictures linking pleasure and rewards to the behavior you want and pain and discomfort to the behavior you want to get rid of. Play these "mental movies" for yourself several times a day, every day. If you really focus your attention on them, you'll be creating new associations in your brain, associations that will make it much easier for you to change your behavior in a lasting, positive way all in the form of

Affirmations

Let's go back now and remember how your self-image has been constructed. We talked about the concept of self-talk and how you think and we said we talk in three dimensions. That three-dimensional form of thought, as you are speaking and describing to yourself, is being recorded in the neuron of your brain.

What you're going to do is take charge, take control, over the changes that you want to make. You are not going to allow it to happenstance, or maybe; but you're going to deliberately, intentionally say to yourself ... "I want this kind of an attitude. I want to change this kind of behavior. I want to stretch my comfort zone. I want to be able to go far beyond where I allow myself to go."

> **As you visualize the new, you become dissatisfied with the old.**

Think about ways you would like to free flow your behavior. You don't need to consciously think about it. You can just let go and flow at the new level of excellence that you have a desire to be. Here's the kind of imagery that changes the inside you. It is experiential, first person, present tense, and positive. I just keep seeing end results and assimilating the end results into me, letting my subconscious create the how.

The affirmations are not an end result. The affirmations are a means to get you the end result. The affirmation process is to change the construct in your brain. Once you've decided the change you want, writing it out is very important; but every affirmation will be only one sentence long, not a paragraph. It's got to be one sentence. When you write them out, this is personal. If somebody else was to read them, then it would sound selfish. I can't affirm for you, I can only affirm for me; so it will sound like "I am ..." or "I have ..." or "It's easy for me." See, it's personal.

The second step is, it's positive. I want to create the picture I'm moving toward. I want to create an idea for my mind that causes me to seek it, positive.

Present-Tense. All it simply means is all of your goals, like the way you're going to speak when you finish reading this book, is as though you already are, or you already have what it is you're seeking. It's the future in the present tense. It's the future in the present tense.

Achievement. See, sometimes people say I can be a good person. I can or I will. I can be nice; I'm just not. I can is only speaking of your potential, not of the result. Do you see the difference? You're speaking about the potential inside of yourself when you say, "I can." But the harsh truth is that sometimes you look around and that's not the reality you see. Wow, you've got a problem, and you're supposed to.

No comparison. Comparing yourself, being better than, greater than is not at all going to help you be successful. What it is then, is I want you to observe others. Use others as a model. Take their attributes and assimilate those into yourself like you'd like to have them. But remember, you're building a better you.

Action words. It's moving pictures in real life, so you put in words like, "I quickly," "I easily," "I fluently," "I aggressively," because you want your pictures to move.

Emotion words. The power comes in the emotion. You put in an appropriate emotion. "It makes me feel proud to be ..." "It brings great joy ..." "I feel enthusiastic about ..." The more emotion, the faster the change.

Accuracy. I'm going to lose some weight. Clarity, exactness, being explicit is what you need. You'll have trouble forcing yourself, I know, to be clear. Why do you suppose people would have difficulty being clear? It makes you accountable. If you can't get any clearer, it's because either you haven't spent the time to focus or you're dodging accountability.

Balance. It's important when you start out goal setting ... It is essential because you're going to run obsessively with this process. You're going to become obsessive, inside yourself. You're going to drive yourself like you've never been driven before. What's Realistic? I don't know, but there is a limit, because you can't take yourself past what you can imagine yourself doing. Don't worry about that, just get started. Then as you start approaching your goal, you can set the goal, and go past it.

Confidential. By the way, you've got to keep your Affirmations confidential. You can't go telling everybody. For a variety of reasons, confidentiality is very important. If you tell somebody you're going to do it, it's going to become a "have to" goal. You force yourself into it, and you work against it. You don't need to be pushed into or forced into change; you want to grow into it. Confidentiality — only with those people who will support your growth.

Now, sometimes change is just a thought for you. "Wouldn't that be nice ...", and then you forget about it. And you will forget about it; I'll tell you why. Because your creative subconscious has the job of sustaining this image as you are now. With this process of affirmations, you are messing around with this creative subconscious. This creative subconscious will try to make you forget that you wanted to change. It will find excuses for you to not change. Its job is to sustain the reality that you have in the neuron of your brain.

This is a deliberate technique which works. It's scientific. It's not anything I thought up. You write it out so that every time you read the words, it takes you in your forethought into the circumstance of the situation as though you actually are. We're not leaving it to chance. You're deliberately deciding, maybe 12 to 15 to 20 changes you're going to make at a time. You're going to intentionally and deliberately script it out.

Now, when you write these affirmations out, that does not make the change. That's just the beginning. Now, just before you fall asleep at night is the best natural time to give your mind the new image and the new emotion. Because you are close to what is called the alpha state of consciousness. The day-dreaming state is when you're most receptive to your own suggestion. Then, when you awaken in the morning before you get into the spin of your day is your second-best time. You're closest to the alpha state of consciousness, the daydreaming state.

The more emotion, the faster the change.

I want you to take the time to deliberately program into your mind the new image, the new picture, and the new emotion that you're going to have guiding your behavior – until you choose to change it again. The process, once you have written your affirmations, is to read the words of your affirmation. Then close your eyes and get an image or a picture of where you would be with your family, friends, or work. Let those words take you into that circumstance.

Then take the emotion that you want carried, and you will write your affirmation so it describes the kind of emotion you want to carry forward into that circumstance. You read, picture, and feel the emotion. Then you go to your second affirmation; read, picture, and feel. Then go to your third, fourth, and so on. That's all it takes.

It should be harder, don't you think? Don't you think it should be more difficult than that? It's not, but what you must do is be clear on the specific changes that you choose to make. You keep altering and changing the automatic pilot system, which is your subconscious. It is your internal idea of who you are and how you are. As you change, don't try hard to be what you're affirming. Don't pretend you are what you told yourself to be.

Here's what you do. Observe your behavior. You want to reflect back over the morning or the afternoon or the end of the day. Reflect back even while you're performing, if it's athletics or singing, or if it happens to be something socially. You will be able to observe your behavior. I'm going to write a little cycle for you to remember. You have your self-image, which is your idea of how you are. That image controls your performance reality or how you act. When you don't consciously control it, it's how you act. But what human beings do is observe how you just behaved, and with your self-talk you describe to yourself what you've observed.

If your behavior is unwanted, you just keep telling yourself, "Well, there I go again. That's like me. I've always been that way." This reinforces the self-image and makes you act like that again. What you must do is intercept your self-talk. When you see your behavior like your old behavior that's unwanted, here's what I want you to tell yourself, "I'm better than that now. That's no longer like me. That's not like me any longer." You then will tell yourself, and this is the key phrase, "The next time I intend to ..." Then you give yourself your affirmation with your self-talk. Otherwise, what you say to yourself, "There I go again. That's like me. I've always been that way." All you do is reinforce your old behavior, your old emotion that's unwanted, your old performance level.

You must correct it with your self-talk. "That is not like me. I am better than that. No more." Now you must give yourself a replacement picture. It's all about replacement pictures. The replacement picture statement for you is, "The next time ..." You tell yourself how you're going to treat that person, how brave you're going to be, how you're going to make that happen, whatever it was you wanted to have happen. So you're going to carefully select, in your mind, the image you want inside your mind.

When your behavior is less, when your performance is less, when your response is unwanted now, you must tell yourself, "I'm better than that." Your self-talk is going to come back to you and say, "Well, you've always been this way. Who are you fooling?" You can say to yourself, "Maybe up until now, but no more." You're going to get tough with yourself. Never make the mistake that being positive is weak, soft, and permissive. You're telling yourself the exact picture you want in the future. You're changing your mind. You're not going to let the old pictures dominate your behavior. Although it presently is, you must give yourself a new picture to seek. You are a seeker. Because you seek images, if you don't give yourself a new picture, you will go back to your old picture.

Then every day, you are going to be very conscious of your self-talk, and you're going to be very conscious of your behavior. You're going to watch. When you are successful at the level with which you've chosen, here's what you're going to say to yourself, "Yes! That's like me. That is like me. I'm really good at this. Yes, this is like me." When you see yourself performing at the level with which you were affirming, then you must reaffirm yourself. That's how you grow.

Dr. Albert Bandura of Stanford University, the best in the world in cognitive research, tells us that most people pass through their accomplishments too quickly and too lightly to have them make any change in their current image of reality. Now, what would that look like? Well, here's something successful. You may have said to yourself, "Oh, it was nothing. I had nothing to do with it. Oh, well, it was an accident." You must elevate your image.

You've got to raise your image of yourself. You've got to alter the picture to a whole new level.

You must reiterate it when you are doing something successful. You've got to remember it. You've got to reflect on it. You've got to assimilate it. You've got to let yourself feel it. You see, that's what high performance people do. They let themselves feel their success. When you are successful, even with little things (it doesn't need to be big things, just little changes), say, "Yes! Yes, I'm changing. I see it. I feel it. Yes. Look at that, there I am." That's the way you want to talk to yourself.

When your performance is beneath what is normal for what you want to be, remember you are creating a new normal from what you used to be. When your performance is beneath what you are seeking, you must tell yourself, "No more! I'm better than that. That's no longer like me." Then you affirm again the next time, and you take yourself into the future.

You see yourself the next time performing at this level or responding with this emotion. That's all there is to it. But when you are successful, again, what must you tell yourself? "Yes! Wow, yes, that's like me. That's like me." Every high-performance person does that. They do it automatically. They don't even know they're doing it.

If you sit by your children's bedside before they fall asleep at night, what should you ask them? I suggest, "What did you do today? What went so well?" What you're getting them to do with their self-talk is to reaffirm something they did great. It elevates their image of who they are. It raises their self-image, their self-esteem. You're borrowing a great emotion of the past and coloring your future expectation. You see how that works? You do that every night.

Before long, you'll see yourself and say, "Wow, my gosh." People around you are going to say, "You really are different."

Now when they tell you, you are different, subconsciously it may bother you. You say, "Oh, well..." People are going to say, "When are you going to be your old self? When are you going to quit faking it?

Who are you trying to impress?" See, they're going to see you differently. You're changing their reality. Your family is going to see you differently. Your close friends are going to see you acting differently. You're changing their reality, and they're going to try to pull you back. Don't let them. You're on your journey. You're on your way to going far beyond your normal.

This process is not something I made up. It is very scientifically documented, but it's also just the way people grow naturally. You're going to do it intentionally. Got it?

I'm going to do something very significant for you that I have not seen done anywhere before. I will teach you during the remainder of this chapter how to write actual admirations and give you a few examples of affirmations I personally used over the years. This is your BONUS piece to this chapter. Enjoy!

Affirmations Workshop

In this bonus section, you'll learn how to write affirmations and practice writing them. You will use the goal ideas you have worked on. An affirmation is a statement of fact or belief. When written correctly, an affirmation will trigger a picture in your mind of your goal already accomplished.

Your affirmations are your tools to deliberately control your own forethought. As you have learned, this is how successful, high – performance people win so frequently. You can paint your own positive scenarios, change your picture on the inside first, and automatically gravitate to word your goals by using these tools.

There are 11 basic guidelines for writing affirmations. Review them closely.

1. **Personal:** Affirmations are written with the word "I" in them. You can only affirm for yourself. The desired change will, come about because of something you do, and it is your own inner picture that will change because of your affirmation.

2. **Positive:** always describe what you want in your affirmation. Describe what you want to move toward, not what you want to move away from. What would it look like if it were fixed?

3. **Present Tense:** affirmations are written as though they are happening right now. This requires using your imagination and becomes easier with practice.

4. **Indicate Achievement:** Eliminate words such as, "can, will, should, want to" from your affirmations. Include phrases such as, "I am, I do, I have." It is important to give your subconscious a clear picture of the end result as though it is already accomplished.

5. **No Comparisons**: Comparing yourself to others is ineffective. The technique of affirming is a personal process. Your measurement of growth is based on yourself.

6. **Action Words:** Use terms that describe and trigger action pictures, such as "easily, quickly, thrive on, energetically, confidently," in your affirmations.

7. **Emotion Words:** These are of critical importance. The more positive emotion you feel when picturing your accomplished goal, the faster your affirmation will work for you.

8. **Accuracy:** If your goal is to exercise regularly, what kind of exercise? Is it jogging, walking, swimming, aerobics, or something else? How regularly? Three times a week? If so, on what days? What time of day and for how long? This is how accurate your affirmations must be. If written in general terms, the picture is too vague and gives you too many escape routes.

9. **Balance:** Set goals and write affirmations in all areas of your life.

10. **Realistic:** After you have written your affirmation, close your eyes and picture. Can you see yourself there? You need to be able to see it, visualize it, and imagine it.

11. **Confidential:** Share your affirmations with only those you are certain will support and help you achieve them. Most of your personal affirmations need not be shared.

Choose your Action/Emotion words to LIST HERE:

Write all the positive action emotion words you like from your vocabulary. I provided an extensive list for you below.

_____

_____

_____

_____

_____

_____

_____

_____

_____

_____

_____

Action/Emotion Words

Accepted
Accomplish
Achieve
Acknowledge
Active
Adaptable
Admire
Adorable
Adventurous
Affectionate
Agreeable
Aggressive
Alert
Amazing
Ambitious
Articulate
Aspiring
Assertive
Assured
Attentive
Beautiful
Beloved
Blessed
Blissful
Brave
Bright
Brilliant
Calm
Capable
Caring
Charming
Cheerful
Clean
Clear
Clever

Colorful
Comfortable
Comic
Compassionate
Competent
Complete
Complementary
Composed
Concise
Confident
Conscientious
Considerate
Constructive
Content
Cooperative
Courteous
Creative
Cultured
Curious
Dazzling
Decisive
Delightful
Dependable
Deserving
Determined
Devote
Dignified
Diligent
Diplomatic
Disciplined
Dramatic
Cook Dutiful
Dynamic
Eager
Easy

Effective
Efficient
Effortless
Electric
Elegant
Eloquent
Embrace
Encouraging
Endearing
Enduring
Energetic
Enjoyable
Enlightened
Enterprising
Entertaining
Entrusted
Enthusiastic
Excellent
Exceptional
Exciting
Expectant
Expressive
Faithful
Famous
Fantastic
Fascinating
Fearless
Feminine
Fervent
Festive
Flexible
Fluent
Forceful
Forgiving
Fortunate

Fresh	Important	Marvelous
Friendly	Impressive	Meaningful
Frugal	Independent	Mellow
Fulfilling	Individualistic	Melodious
Fun	Industrious	Memorable
Gallant	Influential	Merry
Generous	Ingenious	Mighty
Genial	Innovative	Modest
Gentle	Inspiring	Moral
Genuine	Inspirational	Motivated
Gifted	Instrumental	Musical
Giving	Intellectual	Myself
Glad	Intelligent	Natural
Glorious	Intense	Neighborly
Good	Intentional	Noble
Graceful	Intuitive	Nourishing
Gracious	Inventive	Obedient
Grammatical	Jolly	Obliging
Grand	Jovial	Outstanding
Great	Joyous	Passionate
Growing	Jubilant	Patient
Handy	Just	Patriotic
Happy	Kind	Peaceful
Harmonious	Knowing	Perceptive
Healthy	Knowledgeable	Persevering
Hearty	Learned	Personable
Helpful	Likable	Placid
Honest	Lively	Pleasant
Honorable	Lovable	Pleasing
Hospitable	Lovely	Pleasurable
Humble	Loving	Polite
Humorous	Loyal	Positive
Idealistic	Lucky	Powerful
Illustrious	Luminous	Practical
Immense	Lyrical	Praiseworthy
Impartial	Magnetic	Precise
Impeccable	Magnificent	Prepared

Presentable
Prestigious
Principled
Privileged
Productive
Professional
Proficient
Progressive
Promising
Prosperous
Proud
Prudent
Punctual
Pure
Purposeful
Qualified
Quick
Quiet
Quotable
Radiant
Rapid
Rational
Realistic
Reasonable
Receptive
Refined
Refreshing
Regal
Relaxed
Reliable
Reputable
Resourceful
Respectable
Respected
Respectful
Responsible
Retentive

Reverent
Rich
Safe
Scholarly
Secure
Seeing
Seeking
Selective
Self – confident
Self – contained
Self – reliant
Sensational
Sensible
Sensitive
Sentimental
Serene
Sharing
Significant
Simply
Sincere
Skillful
Smiling
Smart
Smooth
Sociable
Sophisticated
Sparkling
Special
Spectacular
Speedy
Spirited
Spiritual
Splendid
Spontaneous
Sporting
Stable
Stalwart

Steadfast
Steady
Strong
Strengthen
Stylish
Stunning
Sturdy
Successful
Super
Superb
Supportive
Sure
Survivor
Swift
Sympathetic
Systematic
Tactful
Teachable
Tender
Terrific
Thankful
Thorough
Thrifty
Thriving
Timely
Tireless
Tolerant
Tranquil
Treasured
Thoughtful
Triumphant
True
Trusted
Trustworthy
Trustful
Understanding
Unforgettable

Universal
Uplifting
Useful
Valiant
Valuable
Venturesome
Vibrant
Victorious
Vigorous
Virtuous
Visible
Visionary
Visual
Vital
Vivacious
Vivid
Warm
Wealthy
Welcome

Well
Willing
Wholesome
Winner
Winning
Wonderful
Working
Worthwhile
Worthy
Young
Youthful
Zealously
Zestful

Words to Avoid

Better
But
Can
Could
Even if
Going to
Have to
Hope to
Less
Maybe
Might
Wish
Would
Would like to

More
Need to
Never
Not
Should
Some
Something
Try
Want to
Will

Sample Affirmations:

Personal   Emotional

⇕   ⇕

I *thrive* on my **daily** jogging because I feel *healthy/strong/energetic*.

⇕   ⇕

Action   Accurate/Realistic

The following list has a variety of sample affirmations that may be helpful. Some may fit your career situation, others focus on your personal life, and some may overlap. If some of these affirmations work for you, please use them, but be sure to rewrite them so they are you talking to you.

1. I like and respect myself, because I know that I am a worthy, capable, and valuable person.

2. I enjoy my life and my relationships with other people.

3. I have an excellent, free-flowing memory with clear and easy recall.

4. It is easy and fun to write and imprint affirmations daily.

5. I enjoy making affirmations daily, because of the positive and quick results I get.

6. I have a positive expectancy of success, and I see all setbacks as temporary.

7. I enthusiastically arrive at work on time and attend meetings with an open mind and a positive attitude.

8. I am very effective and efficient, especially in stressful situations.

9. I have pride in my performance and positive expectations of my future.

10. I express myself well, and I know others respect my point of view.

11. I quietly do helpful and worthwhile things for others.

12. I look for ways of uplifting myself and others, and I do it with ease every day.

13. I am accountable for the results of my decisions and actions.

14. I am my own expert, and I accept only positive attitudes and opinions from others.

15. Because of the warmth and love I show my children, I teach them to show warmth and love to each other.

16. I develop feelings of respect and self-esteem in myself and others.

17. Because I sincerely care about myself and the quality of my life, I am financially responsible.

18. My family and friends are benefiting from the successes that have come from my hard work.

19. I am healthy and energetic because I treat my body with the love and respect I deserve.

20. I reinforced my successes and positively correct for errors.

21. Giving presentations in front of my coworkers is fun and uplifting.

22. I speak clearly and calmly and make positive contributions that benefit me and my peers.

23. I am a successful professional and earn $_____per month. I live a comfortable and happy life.

24. Because of our true spirit of intent in leading ourselves and our team, it is easy to empower our people, resulting in extraordinary customer satisfaction.

25. I am fair and just in dealing with people I lead.

26. Because I am well-organized, I enjoy my neat and orderly office.

27. I feel calm and relaxed in potentially stressful situations, seeing all customers' challenges as opportunities in disguise.

Answer the following *LIFE CHANGING & AFFIRMATIONS QUESTIONS* to get you out of your comfort zone before going on to the next chapter:

Grow from Your Comfort-Zone

1. Three areas where I want to make significant change right now are?

_____

_____

_____

_____

_____

_____

_____

_____

_____

_____

_____

_____

_____

_____

_____

_____

_____

_____

2. What do I want these three areas to look like when the change is made? (Use this information in the affirmation workshop exercise from above)

_____

_____

_____

_____

_____

_____

_____

_____

_____

_____

_____

_____

_____

3. In the following areas, I have been successful. What could I do to become significant in these areas as well?

_____

_____

_____

_____

_____

_____

_____

_____

_____

_____

_____

_____

4. In what other areas could I make a significant contribution to my family, relationship, community, and nation?

_____
_____
_____
_____
_____
_____
_____
_____
_____
_____
_____
_____
_____

My Notes:

_____
_____
_____
_____
_____
_____
_____
_____
_____
_____
_____
_____
_____

So if you haven't as yet done so, do not go past this chapter on to chapter twelve. Take an internal inventory of where you are now in your internal conversation process. Work on changing or improving by answering the questions and making your notes about what came up for you while reading chapter eleven. Remember, there is always hope.

You can change, which is the exact reason I believe you bought the Today Is the Day BOOK, RIGHT? So make the changes by starting NOW! When you attend one of our live workshops, we go through each question in depth and I personally hold you accountable before moving on. So even though I'm not there personally reading with you, pretend I'm there now holding you accountable.

Take great comfort in knowing that ALL great feats are accomplished one small step at a time. TAKE THE SMALL STEPS!

They make a BIG difference. I would love to know how it's working for you. I enjoy the comments on my Facebook page (FB.com/obombowen), and I look forward to hearing from you soon. This is probably the simplest way I can help you remain accountable to your continued growth and success.

If you're more like my wife and prefer a hands-on experience, then join us at one of our upcoming workshops. If you're ready to learn how to transform your life, success, or marriage, join the next Today Is the Day workshop, the best life-transforming program. For more information, go to my website (www.todayisthedaybook.com). Give yourself this gift as a reward of investing in your happiness and growth.

CHAPTER TWELVE

It's My Choice

Motivation can be negative and restrictive which causes me to push back, or permissive. Putting my life on a "want-to" basis moves me forward, beyond my present limitations.

Overview

Fear can play a big role in our lives. Fear can keep us safe. Fear can keep us from moving into exciting worlds. Fear can also be used to motivate us, but it's a motivation that ultimately causes tension and stress and unlocks our creativity in order to avoid a problem or situation. Imposed from the outside, or from the inside, fear causes anyone with any level of self-esteem to push back.

Objectives

By the end of this Chapter, you will understand:

- Areas in my life where I let fear hold me back.
- That motivation can be negative and restrictive, which causes need to push back.
- Putting my life on a constructive, "want to" basis moves me forward, beyond my present limitations.

Key Learning Principle

Do what you want to do, and just accept the consequences. Our present thoughts determine our future. If you could change one thing about your life, what would it be? Now, I'm not talking about magic, because some things – such as how tall you are – simply cannot be changed.

But, you know, there really isn't much that you can't alter if you want it badly enough – assuming you know how to go about it, and assuming that you take action as needed. Wanting to badly is a great start, but it won't get you anywhere by itself. Neither will affirmations or visualizations, if that's all you do.

If you want to get started making changes in yourself, pick one thing to begin with. It doesn't matter what it is, as long as it's doable. Then go after it with everything you've got. Visualize how you'll feel and behave after the change is made. Write affirmations to support the visualization and repeat them every day, over and over. Make an action plan with sub-goals and daily and weekly tasks. Make yourself accountable to follow the plan and reward yourself every time you achieve a sub-goal.

Enlist help if you need it and don't worry about how long it takes. If you keep moving toward the end-result you want and keep tracking your progress, you'll get there, believe me. There's an extra added bonus. When you see that you can do it, you'll inspire others – and yourself – to do even more.

There is something very special you're going to need in order to allow yourself to reach the full potential inside of you. This will allow you to be your best. This will allow you to live without fear.

There are two kinds of motivation that I'm going to share. You'll recognize both of them. Remember, motivation is not like getting hyped from the outside. It is the internal drive and energy released from inside of you. That external motivation is artificial and not useful for very long.

The teacher didn't motivate me. The coach didn't motivate. My boss doesn't motivate me. Motivate yourself. How do I do that? I'm going to show you. One type of motivation is based on fear; the other is based on something that you value, want, or love to do. One kind is called coercive, and the other is called constructive. Coercive is always based on fear, and constructive is based on value.

You can always tell when you are being coerced into something because it has these words attached to it, "I have to, or else." The key phrase is, "I have to." I pointed out there were two other words attached to it, "or else." I have to or else I'll lose my job. I have to or else someone will get mad at me. I have to or else something awful is going to happen to me. This mindset is very limited. It is a very fear-based way of motivating yourself.

Do what you want to do, just accept the consequences.

The other is constructive. By seeing the value, why I want to, why I like it, why I choose to. Why I love it. It's my idea. Now many people who have been raised theologically have been taught by their churches or their religion to be good, not necessarily because they want to be good. But they would teach you or encourage you to be good because if you aren't good, you're going to go to hell. Let me tell you what hell looks like. It's fiery down there. Have you ever been thirsty? There is no water forever.

Now, do you want to be good? Yeah. How come? Because I don't want to be going to hell. I'm not going to be good because I want to be good, so you spend your whole life (if you can imagine) out-running the flames of hell licking at your butt.

Fear-based motivation is inhibitive, restrictive, and keeps you from being your best.

If you would look at all the things that you say to yourself you "have" to do. What do you have to do at work? Some of you say, "Oh, I have to be at work between 9am and 5pm. I have to be at work between Monday and Friday, but I really don't want to." Well then quit. See, when you stop and think about it, there's only one thing that you have to do. You have to die. Everything else is really a matter of choice.

Sometimes the choices are not all that good. But if you tell yourself you have to do something, quite frankly you're lying to yourself. You don't have to. You have other options. Nobody can force you to do something against your own will that you don't want. Even if somebody puts a gun to your head and tells you, "You have to run." You don't have to run. Tell them to shoot. I don't want them to shoot. Well then, start running. You don't have to run. You choose to run. You don't have to work here. You choose to work here.

Someone who has children says, "I have to change their diapers." No, you don't. Leave them on. They'll eventually fall off. I don't want to live that way. Well then, shut up and change their diapers. You don't have to. You choose to or you want to. It's your idea. You want to live with free will. You can't defecate your free will because when you do tell yourself you have to do something, you subconsciously resist the coercion whether I'm telling you or you're telling yourself. You have to do your work. You have to do this.

You must learn to tell yourself, "I'm not going to do it if I don't want to." Figure out why you want to do it. All of your goals must be set on a want to, choose to, like it, love it, it's my idea basis. You've got to make it your idea, not somebody else's. If you're working for people who are coercive, you still don't need to live under their coercion. You can do it because you choose to do it, not because they're telling you to do it.

Those of you who are managers of other people, if you are starting to coerce people, you are holding your organization back. Because as you push, they push back. It's easy to remember, so simple. When pushed, people push back. The more self-esteem you have and the higher and stronger you are the more you feel pushed against your will, the more subconsciously you push back.

But you don't push back physically. You push back through procrastination; you slow down, through creative avoidance and you find something else to do. You do the work only good enough to get the person who is pushing to shut up and no more. Never striving for excellence. You can get a whole culture thinking that they 'have to' be at work. I have to do this. I have to do that. Can you imagine how absolutely exhausting that is? I would say in the United States one of the most dangerous places to stand at 5 o'clock at night is in the doorway of a government building. They are there because they have to be there.

They don't care what needs to be done. At 5 o'clock, they are out of there. "I'm out of here" mindset. But if you have people working there because they love what they're doing, then the hours don't mean anything. The energy is flowing; the creativity is flowing, flowing to achieve the objective. It isn't flowing to "get myself out of here."

We work with our special situations just like high-performance athletes do. We must get the coaches to stop coercing their players. That's the old bully way. Coercing people against their will, making them do it because they don't want to it. Have the players want to. If they don't want to, let them quit. If they don't want to quit, watch them. They will attack the future.

They go out playing and asking themselves, "How good can I be? How much can I do?" They don't worry about losing or failing. They're worrying about nothing. All they're thinking about is how good can we be? How much can I do? That's the way I live my life.

I live my life personally on a want to, choose to, like it, love it basis. I'm teaching you not because I have to, but because I want to. It's my idea. My energy and creativity are there. You can tell the difference. If I had to teach, it would sound like it.

This is my life. It wasn't always this way. For a long time I was teaching in the Marine Corps. You just have to do this. You have to go to this training staff meeting. You have to do that. You have to make out training schedules for the unit. Come on.

I do a hundred times more than I ever did before, and it's all because I want to, not because I have to. I live my life on a want to, choose to, like it, love it basis. That's what I want you to do. Watch yourself, eliminate I have to. Put a lot of want to. Quit coercing yourself into things. Change that to a choose-to, want to, like it, and love it. It's your idea. Become accountable, become responsible. You will also see that when you tell yourself you have to do something, you're losing your own respect, which is called self-esteem. Hard to figure that out, isn't it? Because you're saying you're not your own person.

I'm being forced against my will. If I had my way, I'd be doing something else. See I don't have my way, I have to do this. People are making me do this. You lose your own respect for yourself. You don't even know it. It's very subtle. It's all subconscious, and you lose your power. Everything you're going to hear from here forward is all your idea. Choose to, want to, like it, love it.

This is the way you're going to control your self-talk. This is the way you're going to become a great leader. You're going to become the kind of a person that people just love working for. You need to figure out why they want to. You need to be able to persuade. If you want to be able to encourage, you must help people see the value in it for them. What is the personal value in it for them and for you? You want to stress the value and seek it. Stress the value and seek it. Got it?

This next section will be for you to take notes on your thoughts and answer the *POWERFUL LIFE CHANGING QUESTIONS*:

Grow from Your Comfort-Zone

1. What are the "have to" things in my life? In my business? In my relationship?

_____

_____

_____

_____

_____

_____

_____

_____

_____

_____

_____

_____

_____

2. Taken my list of "have to" things, what is the personal value for each "have to" that would allow me to turn them into "want to" things?

_____

_____

_____
_____
_____
_____
_____
_____
_____
_____
_____
_____
_____
_____
_____

3. What can I do to turn my organizations "have to" items into "want to" items? How can I find the personal and organization value that will cause the shift in attitude?

_____
_____
_____
_____
_____
_____
_____
_____
_____
_____
_____
_____

My Notes:

_____
_____

_____

_____

_____

_____

_____

_____

_____

_____

_____

_____

_____

_____

_____

_____

_____

_____

_____

_____

_____

So if you haven't as yet done so, do not go past this on to chapter thirteen. I implore you to take an internal inventory of where you are now. Work on changing or improving. That starts with answering the questions and making your notes about what came up for you while reading chapter twelve. If it's hard to accept where you are, there is always hope. You can change. That's exactly why you got this BOOK. So make the change by starting NOW!

If we accept that sooner rather than later, we would be one step closer to having true happiness and success. The past can sometimes be our adversary because we seem to let it take over and decide our futures. We cannot let the negativity of the past dictate our current lives and futures.

What I love the most about sharing the above information and tips is doing it live with an audience. From the stage, I watch the lightbulbs come on and see others know immediately that it's possible to have true love, success, or the ideal life. It is also amazing doing a radio interview and being able to interact and answer questions from the callers. With my readers, I'm always excited to get comments or questions on my Facebook Fan Page (FB.com/obombowen). Visit anytime and let me know how I can continually be of help or service to you.

I have added an additional bonus for you. You can go to my relationship website: www.globalfairytale.com to download and print a FREE copy of my actual affirmations to serve as a guide for you as you create your own. You will also find so much more on the BONUS tab. I wish for you love and abundance.

To that note in the next chapter, I can't wait to share with you more of the most powerful secrets that will transform and ignite the new you. Lastly, if you're ready to learn how to transform your life, success, or marriage, join the next Today Is the Day workshop, the best life-transforming program. For more information, go to my website (www.todayisthedaybook.com). Give yourself this gift as a reward of investing in your happiness and growth.

CHAPTER THIRTEEN

Yes, I Am Good!

It is time for me to take charge of my estimation of my worth and stop relying on the opinion of others.

Overview

One of the keys to personal and professional success is how we estimate our own worth. How we see ourselves has such a strong influence that we will not even attempt something if we don't think we can achieve it. If an opportunity seems too big for us, we walk away (sometimes, run) from it. Further compromising our ability to grow is that we have a tendency to surround ourselves with others who try to keep us in our "place," and we make the mistake of listening to them.

Objectives

By the end of this chapter, you will understand:

- It is time for me to take charge of my estimation of my own worth and stop relying on the opinion of others.
- That I need to take credit for the successes in my life and give credit to those who have helped me.
- It is a part of who I am to help others raise their opinions of themselves so that the whole is even greater than the sum of its parts.

Key Learning Principle

There is a direct relationship between self-esteem and the way our world works. The family is the main place where we develop our self-esteem. It can also be a place where self-esteem withers. Virginia Satir was a family therapist who influenced and touched people all over the world. She was a pioneer in the study of self-esteem and had this to say about families, "Feelings of worth flourish in an atmosphere where individual differences are appreciated, mistakes are tolerated, communication is open, and rules are flexible – the kind of atmosphere that is found in a nurturing family."

But if you grew up in a family where one or both parents were abusive, where there were unresolved mental health problems, or where alcohol or drugs were an issue, you know that family life can be very different from this description. In fact, it can be downright damaging.

Now it's time for you to take on a parenting role, and maybe you're wondering if you can break the cycle. Or maybe you've been a parent for a while and realize you haven't been doing such a great job. Whatever your situation, you'll benefit from taking an honest look at your strengths and limitations.

You see, when you acknowledge and accept the past, reach out for new understanding (as you're doing now), and decide you'd like to raise your kids in a better way, you are breaking the cycle. And you are building your own self-esteem – the first step in helping your own kids do well.

One of the things that's essential in order to use your potential is to know you are good. Many of you have been raised to not think good of yourself. Many of you've been raised to push away compliments. Many of you've been raised to be humble. But you forgot to look up the definition of humility.

Does humility mean to put yourself down? Does humility mean to push away compliments? "Oh, no, no, no. I'm not good at that. I had nothing to do with that." "My, but you look beautiful." "No, my hair's such a mess. I couldn't possibly ... How could you possibly say I look beautiful?"

Unconsciously what you're doing is pushing away the ability to grow. There's something more about self-esteem which is important, that is you attract the kind of relationships you feel worthy of receiving.

If relationships come to you that you think are too good for you, you will subconsciously somehow push them away. You'll hold them off. You'll delay. You'll stall. You'll associate with people that you can naturally be yourself with. If you go to a party and there are people that you think are too good for you, you can hardly wait to leave and go back with the friends where you can just naturally be yourself.

You are under stress. You are faking it. You are trying hard to be social. You're trying hard to like it here. You also draw to yourself the kind of opportunity and the kind of business that you feel worthy of receiving. If your self-esteem is low and you are actually being considered for promotion, you will do something subconsciously to sabotage your success. Your self-esteem and what is drawn to you in way of relationships and opportunities seem to match.

I want to encourage you. It's very vital and important to raise your opinion of yourself. To elevate your self-esteem, which is a part of your self-concept, your self-image. Self-esteem is your own estimate of your worth. If you wanted to sell your house, would you go out and ask anybody who walks by, "Tell me what my house is worth and I'll sell it?" No. That would be dumb, right? You better go to somebody who can properly evaluate the worth of your house. But many of you let somebody at work tell you what you're worth.

Many of you have let teachers, some of whom should not have been teaching, tell you what you're worth. Many of you will allow people in your social world to tell you what you are worth. So you keep asking and eliciting the approval or the opinion of others because you don't value your own opinion enough. But when you have high self-esteem, you don't need the opinions of others. It's all right if they give them, but your life doesn't sink or rise based upon the opinion of another.

Self-estimate is what self-esteem is. The higher the self-esteem, the higher the performance and the better your life goes. There is a direct correlation between self-esteem and the way your world around you works. Now, you must stop devaluing yourself. I want to encourage you for the next 24 hours to play a game of no put downs, negative affirmations, or "what's the matter with me?" statements. That lowers your esteem. No "how could I have been so stupid?" or "that was stupid of me" remarks that lower your self-esteem, your self-image.

You must eliminate all the sarcasm. Sarcasm is a subtle hostility release. Devaluation of making somebody of less value, making yourself of less value needs to be eliminated. Sarcasm. Belittling. Making somebody lower, be littler than they are. "I know this about her. I know this about him. I don't know why she thinks she's so good. Let me tell you about her." People have a tendency to devalue others to make themselves look better. Rather than growing myself, all I need to do is tell you what's wrong with Betty. "I don't know why Ryan thinks he's so smart; let me tell you where he screwed up."

You're in an environment that is constantly pulling others down. You're in a low self-esteemed environment. Low self-esteemed environments are intimidated by challenges, the future, and the world outside of them. They're stuck in a comfort zone far beneath their potential. So you must think well of yourself.

It's okay to know you're okay. It's essential to know you're okay. You've got to stop waiting for people to tell you that you're good. You've got to tell yourself you're good. You've got to give yourself feedback. You've got to watch when you're improving and tell yourself when you're improving. You've got to see when you're really kind and tell yourself you're kind. You've got to tell yourself when you are brave. You've got to tell yourself when you overcame a risk. You've got to tell yourself that. Because if you don't, you'll never grow. You build your own self-image with your own thoughts.

You've got to stop waiting for other people. Even if other people are telling you, it's up to you to accept it. I could tell you, reader, "You are special. You are wonderful. You are really a delightful person." And you say, "I wonder what he wants? Why is he saying that?" You reject that you could be good. I could also say to one of you, "You are the dumbest or stupidest person I ever worked with." You could say, "You don't look so smart yourself. Who are you to tell me that?"

You have the power to accept or to reject. This is a do-it-yourself project. You've got to raise your own image. Elevate your image. Why? Because then your life gets better. As you elevate your image, your wealth increases and your relationships increase and improve. The world is better based upon your image and your self-esteem level.

That's why, when people pay you a compliment, here's what I recommend. Quit pushing it away. Just say thank you and give credit where credit is due. Give credit to your mother and give credit to God if you believe there's a God. Give credit to your teammates. Give credit to somebody who's helped you, like your teachers or coaches. Did you have anything to do with it? If you did, then accept it. Say thank you.

When you say thank you out loud, inside I want you to say, "Yes! Yes, I'm good. Yes!" What you're doing when you do that is building your image. As you build your image every day, every day find yourself. Catch yourself doing things right and tell yourself so. If you make a mistake, don't say, "There I go again. What's the matter with me anyway?" Tell yourself, "I'm better than that." No more, just tell yourself how you're going to do it the next time.

How you treat people has a lot to do with your self-esteem level. You'll never hear a bad word said about anybody from a high-esteem person. You will find that low self-esteem people are sarcastic, belittling, and devaluing. You can hardly do anything right around them. The wife of a husband with low self-esteem doesn't have a chance. You'll hear comments like, "How do you think you can get a job? You can't even organize the house. Why don't you get down where you belong?" "Where's that?" "Well, below me."

They're constantly finding fault with you to put you in your place. If you're around people like that, you can't accept it. You've got to reject it. "Who are you to tell me that?" You must become a person who disputes those opinions, explanations, and realities that are coming your way. You must become the kind of person who's a people builder that finds the good in others and tells them so.

"I've been meaning to tell you, Linda, how proud I am of you. I've been meaning to tell you how special you are, and here's why I believe so." What you're wanting to do is become a people builder. You escalate the esteem of yourself and the people around you, your whole company. Why? Because there's a direct relationship between performance and how good you think you are.

If you have children, make sure your children are around teachers who have high self-esteem. Otherwise high self-esteem children will be bullied by a low self-esteem teacher. That teacher will be intimidated and threatened by that child and try to put that child in their place. They'll find a way to make him feel stupid or fail. "Oh, that child's cocky. That child thinks too much. He's got an opinion too high." How could you have an opinion too high? It could be incomplete. It could be you don't back it up with what you're doing, but your opinion has got to be high.

It has got to be high. You're not born that way; you develop it. That is why sitting by your child's bedside is so important. You drop them into tomorrow with a positive expectancy. You cover their future with a successful path.

That's a habit of every Special Forces, of every special musician, of every special person. They think that way naturally. You can develop it in your children. You can do that in yourself. You go back and make a list of things you've done well. Allow yourself to dwell on that three or four times a day. Make a list of 5 or 10 things. Think back and dwell on it. Absorb it. Then, take the positive emotion and say, "What's scaring me in the future?"

You color your future with your successful past. You build an emotional future. High-performance people do naturally, and this is who you are becoming. Your life will change so immensely. This is not accidental. It's all intentional and in your mind. It's how you talk or speak to yourself.

Is it worth it? Absolutely. That way you will not intimidated by art teachers like I was. The farthest I would go from my home in New York until I was about 17-years old was 15 miles. I could go from home to Manhattan. I didn't need to go 150 miles. I didn't sit and wait for people to tell me I'm good. I've got to build my own image with my own thoughts. That's what I'm encouraging you to do.

I'll show you how to do that as we go into the next chapter.

Can you do it? Absolutely. Is it essential to do? Absolutely. Now remember, it's all about changing your mind. Why you should change your mind? How do you change your mind? Those are the two most important gifts anybody could ever give you. It's okay to change your mind. It's essential to change your mind. When you change your mind, then your life changes. Your world changes. Your relationships change. You see things differently.

Life is beautiful. Life IS beautiful. Is it sometimes not so good? True. Gosh, there's all kinds of bad things that happen, but this is how you attack the bad things. This is how you deal with the things that aren't good. I have business things that don't go well.

It isn't like everything goes well. I don't quit on it. I'm persistent and resilient. If we look for options, we find ways. We don't accept the opinions of people around us who are doom and gloom. It isn't so much that everything goes perfectly for you – rather, it's how you deal with life that's essential. Does that make sense?

Lastly, the people with whom you associate can have a substantial effect on your self-esteem. How does it make you feel when someone asks how you are, but obviously couldn't care less about your answer? How do you feel when someone who says they care about you belittles your efforts or puts you down?

If you're like most people, things like this hurt your feelings. But did you know that if it happens enough, it could also damage your self-esteem? It's true. It's hard to maintain a high opinion of yourself when those who are closest to you are always trying to pull it down. Of course, the reason they do so in the first place is because of their own poor self-opinion, not because there's anything wrong with you. But when you're experiencing their judgments and criticisms, it can be hard to keep this in mind.

Obviously, if you have a choice, you want to stay away from these kinds of people – the ones who are always evaluating how you look, how well you do things, how moral you are, how witty you seem, and letting you know that you never quite measure up.

I have found that the best people to associate with are those who do two important things at the same time. They act as a mirror that reflects your good points while accepting you just as you are. They also expect excellence from you and continually encourage you to use your full potential. In other words, they see the good in you that sometimes you don't even see, and they tell you about it often.

These are the people that bring out the greatness in others and these are the people you want to make a regular part of your life. Who is that person in your life? Who is the person you need to avoid?

This next section will be for you to take notes on your thoughts and answer the *POWERFUL LIFE CHANGING QUESTIONS*:

Grow from Your Comfort-Zone

1. In what areas of my life does my self-esteem need raising?

_____
_____
_____
_____
_____
_____
_____
_____
_____
_____
_____
_____

2. Here is a list of the 10 things I have done well in my life:

_____
_____
_____
_____
_____
_____
_____
_____
_____
_____
_____
_____
_____

3. As I read over this list of things I have done well, how do I feel? How can I help others in my family and in my organization as well as in my relationship get this same feeling?

_____
_____
_____
_____
_____
_____
_____
_____
_____
_____
_____
_____
_____

4. Where in my organization do we need to raise the level of our collective self-esteem?

_____

_____

_____

_____

_____

_____

_____

_____

_____

_____

_____

_____

5. How can I help do this?

_____

_____

_____

_____

_____

_____

_____

_____

_____

_____

_____

_____

My Notes:

_____

_____

_____

_____

_____

_____

_____

_____

_____

_____

_____

_____

_____

_____

_____

_____

_____

_____

_____

_____

_____

_____

_____

_____

So if you haven't as yet done so, do not go past this on to chapter fourteen. I implore you to take an internal inventory of where you are now. Work on changing or improving.

That starts with answering the questions and making your notes about what came up for you while reading chapter thirteen. If it's hard to accept where you are, there is always hope. You can change. That's exactly why you got this BOOK. So make the change by starting NOW!

If we accept that sooner rather than later, we would be one step closer to having true happiness and success. The past can sometimes be our adversary because we seem to let it take over and decide our futures. We cannot let the negativity of the past dictate our current lives and futures.

What I love the most about sharing the above information and tips is doing it live with an audience. From the stage, I watch the lightbulbs come on and see others know immediately that it's possible to have true love, success, or the ideal life.

It is also amazing doing a radio interview and being able to interact and answer questions from the callers. With my readers, I'm always excited to get comments or questions on my Facebook page (FB.com/obombowen). Visit anytime and let me know how I can continually be of help or service to you.

I have added an additional bonus for you. You can go to my relationship website: www.globalfairytale.com to download and print a FREE copy of my actual affirmations to serve as a guide for you as you create your own. You will also find so much more on the BONUS tab.

I wish for you love and abundance. To that note in the next chapter I can't wait to share with you more of the most powerful secrets that will transform and ignite the new you. Lastly, if you're ready to learn how to transform your life, success, or marriage, join the next Today Is the Day workshop, the best life-transforming program. For more information, go to my website (www.todayisthedaybook.com). Give yourself this gift as a reward of investing in your happiness and growth.

CHAPTER FOURTEEN

Goal Setting Through

In order to keep from flattening out, I need to reset my goals as I approach their accomplishment which keeps me constantly moving forward.

Overview

We have learned how throwing our system out of order by goal setting causes us to create drive and energy to restore order. Now we will learn how to continually create drive and energy, so we grow continuously throughout our lives.

Objectives

By the end of this chapter, you will understand:

- In order to keep from flattening out, I need to reset my goals as I approach their accomplishment.
- It is OK to flatten out or shutdown, but I want to do it by intent, not because I neglected to reset my goal.

Key Learning Principle

Once you arrive at a goal you set, you lose your drive and energy. How important is mental preparation when it comes to achieving a goal within your reach? When you decide on a goal you want to achieve, when you know it is possible, and you feel strongly committed to getting it done, what is next? What can you do that will help ensure positive results?

Well, the first thing you need to do is remind yourself not to get bogged down in figuring out "how" you are going to achieve it. The "how" is important, but it doesn't come first. First, you want to clearly and vividly visualize the end result. The more clearly and more often you see it (and when I say "see it," I mean feel it, taste it, smell it, and make it 100% real in your imagination), the more likely it is to become real in the world.

It takes energy to create reality from a vision or idea, but it happens all the time. Every single person-made reality in the world first started out as an idea inside someone's head. The more thought, the more energy – and the more energy, the more likely the reality.

Professional athletes know this and use visualization techniques all the time. I've been teaching it for more than 23 years. Now, there is research accumulating to back it up. Nowadays these techniques are used in medicine, psychology, and education by more and more folks just like you and me.

Where the thought goes, energy flows. If you can clearly see it, you are far more likely to really be it. Keep that in mind as you move toward your goals. When you set goals for yourself in one area, do you check to see how they fit with goals in other areas? Let's talk about goal-setting for a well-balanced life.

When you think about growing as a person, there are many distinct areas you can consider. Do you want to grow as a spouse or parent, in your social relationships, in your job or career? What about your physical and mental health, your intellectual pursuits, your spiritual life? You can also grow in the things you do for fun or in your involvement with your community.

Did you ever know someone who put so much energy into growth in one or two areas that they ignore or neglect the others? This is what you want to avoid. A good way to stay both on track and in balance is to write out goals for every distinct area in your life. While you are at it, check to be sure that your goals fit together in a consistent manner.

For example, you have a goal to become a better father. However, your career and personal goals take you away from home a great deal or leave you too preoccupied to function well when you are at home. You might want to take another look at your priorities and adjust your balance.

Where the thought goes, energy flows.

This is a good way to help you clarify your values too. Make a list of your values and match them to your list of goals. Do they match or is there unbalance? What is most important to your life? Why? Is that where most of your time, energy, and attention are going? Do you feel that your goals are helping you become a well-balanced person? (Feel free to go back to Chapter 11 and review the affirmation process as use them to help with your goals.)

You've heard me talk about human beings being teleological. Let's just go back and reflect on what that means. It means you're a seeker of objects, a goal seeker. If you have a rocket or a missile, and you direct it toward the heat of an aircraft, it seeks the heat of the aircraft, but the aircraft is moving.

Inside the missile is a guidance system telling it where it is in relationship to where it wants to end up. It asks the question, "Where am I?" As it sees itself off the path of the target, it takes corrective action. "Whoops, too far to the right," and it starts to direct itself back to the left. Then it says, "Whoops, too far to the left," and it comes back to the right.

Most of the time is off the beam or off the target. That's how a teleological mechanism works. It also tells itself, "Whoops, too low. Whoops, too high." It's got to do that in order to maneuver. It's different than an arrow. You release the arrow. If the target moves, it cannot correct. A teleological mechanism is always correcting itself, but it also needs a target to seek.

Let's suppose you've neglected to give yourself a new target to seek. You've neglected to tell yourself anything about what you desire in your personal or business future. It's essential as a human being to have a goal or you die. Death occurs if you don't have one. You will subconsciously reproduce the image of what you have done in the past. That becomes your goal, to reproduce the way your life is, not the way it can be.

You guide on the image that you already have – through neglect or even abdicating to somebody else, "Tell me what I should do with my life. The manager will tell me. The boss will tell me. My friends will tell me. My parents will tell me what I should be doing or what I could be doing." It isn't even your goal. It could be somebody else's goal that you've assimilated.

If you don't give yourself a new picture, you become very susceptible to the suggestions of others. It's your choice to either decide, "I'm going to choose the way I want my life to go," or "I will abdicate and allow others to choose the way my life will go," or "I will just recreate the way it presently is in my own mind." That's how our mind works. You must have a goal. Remember, it's all about replacement pictures also.

You've got to give yourself a replacement picture for your present status quo, for your present comfort zone. Did you deliberately and intentionally put in the comfort zone with which you are now living, the stores you go into, the restaurants, the way that you live your life, or was that just done because it happened to be what the people around you were doing? I can remember I did have some goals, but I was trapped in a comfort zone. I was trapped by the peers around me.

As a child, I was raised in a poor, low-income family. I left my home where I was living with my father in South America when I was thirteen years old. I moved to live with my mother and three other brothers in a one-bedroom apartment in Brooklyn, New York.

I was a foreigner and my cousins were foreigners. I loved that, but we had no full concept of this new world. We had no friends. We had no tribe. We were way out of our comfort zones. I loved it. That was okay, and perhaps that would've been my life had I not also lived in the city and saw that there was a better way than staying at home and playing video games.

What I started doing was setting goals. I wanted to be a Marine, which was about as big as I could think. Nobody ever went to college or university from my family because they were all foreigners and needed to work to find a way in the new country fast. They didn't need college they said, and so the value of education was low.

My mind was, "I want to be like the people I admire. I want to be like my brothers, the ones who joined the military. They were tough, and I loved it as a kid. That would've stopped my reality had I not changed my picture. Had I not, I would still be perhaps a Marine or a military contractor.

Then I decided to be a business coach and a Marine, and so that image was very strong in my mind. I allowed that image to make me go to university for the first time. I began to take classes and then went to university while still serving as a Marine. In the meantime, at the age of nineteen my first wife and I got married and started raising my family. My whole comfort zone was to be a Marine.

I became a very good Marine. I was teaching some of this in the Marine Corps that I am teaching you now. I was becoming a very good business coach but in a confining income level of about eleven hundred dollars a month. My social world was a world of just Marines and a few relatives. The cycle of poverty would have kept me there had I let it; the only way to change was to get away from my home where I was living.

That was my comfort zone. I could've lived that out had I not used and found this imagery and information. Then I decided, "Could I raise my income? Could I expand my relationships?" It was scary to even think about it. I didn't know how to do it, but I started visualizing in my mind doubling my income.

That's as far as I could see. Now, I didn't know how to double my income, but your subconscious is a genius. If you can envision the goal or the lifestyle and create it so it's dominant, then you start inventing ways.

One thing I needed to do was become a very good Marine, and I was for several years in the military system. Then I outgrew the military system. The injuries I sustained in Iraq were a big wake up call.

I could just feel, "There's something bigger for me than where I am now." That "bigger for me" was to go into business for myself, take my classroom to the world. I left with zero dollars in the bank, two children, and my ex-wife to pay child support to. Needless to say, I ended up living out of my car for five years. That's what I had at the time in using this information.

I went and left, and it was scary. But I visualized myself safely, then I went beyond, to where now we're all over the world. We have businesses in South Africa, Tokyo, and London. We have businesses in Latin America. You see, I needed to leave and keep growing.

I didn't just jump from where I was to where I am. It was a gradual process of constantly deciding how big I wanted to go, but I'm never really qualified when I set the goal. I set the goal and I get qualified. I don't wait until I'm qualified. I set the goal, and then by setting the goal correctly, it makes me study, develop, and find new ways of doing things.

Most people are trapped in their own reality that many didn't really give themselves in the first place. It was what your uncles did, it was what your aunts did. It was what your parents did. It was what the people who lived around you were doing, and you aspired to those aspirations without taking yourself way out of your comfort zone.

Now, remember, the container of your reality is in your mind. That image in your mind of the way things are supposed to be causes you to subconsciously release enough energy to maintain that comfort zone day after day after day, but it doesn't give you more energy than you need. It only gives you enough energy to maintain the status quo which is in your mind of the way things are and what's good enough.

The container that you have, which is your image of the way you live in the neuron of your brain, releases enough creativity to maintain the status quo, but no more. It doesn't need to give you more creativity, so most people sit and wait for ideas in order to set a big goal. You set a big goal and you get the ideas. That's the way your mind works.

Your expanded awareness, your awareness of resources and people and what you need is confined by the image you hold in your mind. Your reticular activating system is gathering enough information or resources to maintain your present picture, but no more. If you expand it, then you get more energy, more creativity, and your awareness expands. Then you expand it again and get more. You expand it again and get more. You expand it again and get more.

You've got to have the faith that your mind is a genius. You've got to know that what I'm teaching you is scientifically proven. It is how your mind works. You are not trapped because of your potential or your aptitude. You're trapped because of the image you hold in your mind of how much you expect of your life. So, give yourself a new target, a new goal. If the goal is dominant (and it must be dominant), that goal in the future must be dominant because now the energy inside of you propels you towards that dominant image.

If where you are launching yourself from your present reality is too dominant, then the more you move away, the more disharmony you feel. "I'm off the beam. I'm off target." Which target? "My old one. My old one is pulling me back."

Your guidance system is telling you, "Wow, wherever I'm going and whatever I'm doing is pulling me away from the reality with which I'm secure." You feel negative as you start to lose weight, as you move away from your social world and environment. You get the tension that tells you, "Go back. Go back. Go back."

Once you arrive at a goal that you set, you lose your drive and energy.

By making your future aspiration big and strong and dominant, then what you're doing is becoming dissatisfied with where you're living. You become dissatisfied with your income, and what you're doing is using your creativity that says, "You're off the beam by staying home; you're off the beam by staying a high school teacher. You're bigger than that. Leave it." "Where am I going? I've got to have a clear destination. Where am I going? I must have a clear destination." You can either let somebody else tell you what to do, or you can tell you what to do.

One very important principle: once you arrive at the goal that you have set, you lose your motivation, creativity, and awareness. Go beyond it. When you're out of order and create order back together, like a light switch, your energy shuts off. Just as surely as you turn the lights out, your energy shuts off and your ideas shut off and your awareness shuts down.

If you want examples, it's like people who have worked hard during the day and their goal was just to get home and have dinner. You used your forethought only to take you that far to the end of the day and to have dinner. Watch yourself. Have you ever been so exhausted after dinner that you tell your spouse, "Just throw a blanket over me right here in this chair! I don't have enough energy to get up and go to bed," or you could tell yourself, "You're working hard through Monday to Friday," but you don't tell yourself what you want to do on the weekend. Your weekend comes and you're exhausted, you have nothing to do. Your system is just exhausted. You say, "I must be working too hard." Is it too hard, or you didn't tell yourself what you wanted to do?

You've got to goal set through and not up to the situation. When you goal set to get employed, you probably do nothing except keep up the status quo. A lot of people's goals was to get hired. It could be in some places where you have a lifetime of employment, so it doesn't matter what you do. You've been hired, and you don't even think about growing, expanding, or becoming. "I got hired," and now you get in the way of the growth of the organization. Some of you have the goal to get married and wonder why your marriages go flat; because you don't set another goal in your marriage. You just flatten out. You lose the romance, passion, and life. You can't understand what happened. "Why did we go flat?"

People who set a goal to open a business go bankrupt. Why? Because they didn't set a goal to be profitable. The goal was to open a business. Some people set a goal to go to university, but they didn't set a goal to study. "Oh, I forgot that."

You can either choose to keep resetting goals or you can live out the rest of your life in dull boredom in a state of just stagnation.

Right now, it's important to recognize your future isn't in your hands. Your future is in your mind. Your future could look just like it was yesterday or last year or the year after. Forty years from now some of you will say, "Things haven't changed hardly at all. Life is dull." Yes, you've made it so. You're always wanting to tell yourself, "There is a horizon past this horizon." You've got to be thinking in a way of abstract one level beyond, one level above. You're taking yourself, you're living where you are now, and what you're doing in your mind is taking yourself into a bigger and greater future. You don't need to do that in every part of your life, but in those parts of your life where you want to improve and grow, it's all up to you. It's in your mind.

You must change your mind or don't expect things to happen any differently for you. You can temporarily change something, but you always go back to the dominant idea and the dominant ways that are stored in the neuron of your brain emotionally, habitually, and in your picture of who you are. It's all about changing your mind. Stay tuned – I'm going to teach you how.

Answer the following POWERFUL LIFE CHANGING QUESTIONS:

Grow from the Comfort-Zone

1. When have I lost my drive and energy, before accomplishing a goal? (Personally? Organizationally? Relationally?)

_____

_____

_____

_____

_____

_____

_____

_____

_____

_____

_____

_____

_____

_____

2. Considering the goals I am setting now, which ones might need to be reset in order for me to accomplish my desired end results?

_____

_____

_____

_____

_____

_____

_____

_____

_____

_____

_____

_____

3. What is the next abstract level for me? Where do I want to go?

_____

_____

_____
_____
_____
_____
_____
_____
_____
_____
_____
_____
_____
_____

My Notes:

_____
_____
_____
_____
_____
_____
_____
_____
_____
_____
_____
_____
_____
_____
_____
_____
_____
_____
_____
_____

So if you haven't as yet done so, do not go past on to chapter fifteen. I implore you to take an internal inventory of where you are now. Work on changing or improving. That starts with answering the questions and making your notes about what came up for you while reading chapter fourteen. If it's hard to accept where you are, there is always hope. You can change.

That's exactly why you got this BOOK, RIGHT? So make the change by starting NOW! When you attend one of our live Today Is the Day workshops, we go through each question in depth, and I personally hold you accountable before moving on. So even though I'm not there reading with you personally, pretend I'm there now holding you accountable.

Take great comfort in knowing that ALL great feats are accomplished one small step at a time. TAKE THE SMALL STEPS! They make a BIG difference. I would love to know how it worked for you; I enjoy the comments on my Facebook page (FB.com/obombowen), and I look forward to hearing from you soon. This is probably the simplest way I can help you remain accountable to your continued growth and success.

If you're more hands on like my wife, then join us at one of our upcoming workshops. If you're ready to learn how to transform your life, success, or marriage, join the next Today Is the Day workshop, the best life-transforming program. For more information, go to my website (www.todayisthedaybook.com).

Give yourself this gift as a reward of investing in your happiness and growth. The greatest gift my wife and I have ever given ourselves is attending 4 growth and leadership and marriage retreats per year since 2010. We still do it to this day; you can never stop growing or investing in yourself.

Some interesting information came across my desk recently, and I'd like to share it with you, along with some personal reflections. We are well past the excitement of the new century, but did you know the death rates in the month of January 2000 were higher than any January before? It seems that many desperately ill people set goals to live long enough to see the 21st century. Through sheer force of will, they extended their lives. Once the goal was reached, they let go and pass on.

Charles Schulz, creator of the "Peanuts" comic strip died on February 12, 2000, the night before the publication of his final Sunday strip. His son claimed it was no coincidence. "He had done what he wanted to do, and that was it for him." Now, I don't mean this to be depressing. We've all known or heard of people who willed themselves to either live or die. You see, we are dealing with the strongest entity on earth — the human mind.

My question to you is this: If one can goal set to live or die, what else can we be goal setting to accomplish? If the mind has the power of life and death, what is holding us back?   NO REALLY??? Write it in below and start to change it TODAY!

_____

_____

_____

_____

_____

_____

_____

_____

_____

_____

_____

_____

_____

_____

_____

CHAPTER FIFTEEN

Successful and Significant

Yesterday's dreams are today's necessities. Today's dreams are tomorrow's opportunities!

Overview

We have learned that words trigger pictures, which then trigger emotions or how we feel to work the pictures we hold in our minds. This is powerful knowledge in understanding how we think affects our performance, because we move toward what we think about. When we think about how things used to be, we are stuck in the past. When we focus on how things are today, nothing changes. However, when we imagine what we would like for the future, we are wrong to that future.

Objectives

By the end of this chapter, you will understand:

- I am drawn to the pictures I hold in my mind, of the way things are and how I would like them to be.
- That in order to move forward with my work and business, I need to look around the challenges in front of me and create pictures of the future I want.

Key Learning Principle

Intentional living is about living a life of significance. But what does "significance" mean? Here's how I look at it: "Success" happens when we achieve something for us – in other words, when we hit a personal goal, one that we have set for ourselves. It could be to lose weight, exercise more, get to work earlier, or even a goal for our team such as a revenue or profitability goal. It's when we achieve something we want to do – that's success.

"Significance" is when we help someone else succeed. Once you taste significance, success will no longer cut it.

One of my favorite "Today Is the Day" workshop exercises is when I ask leaders to think of someone who has had a major impact on them – someone who has really helped them breakthrough or grow. Once they have a clear image of who that is, I ask what it was about that person who made such a difference. These are consistently the top three traits I hear:

1. **They cared about me.** Zig Ziglar got it right 30+ years ago when he said: "People don't care how much we know until they know how much we care."

2. **They listened. Think about that – the simple act of listening.** Why do we have so much struggle listening when it means so much to those with whom we want to make a difference?

3. **They believed in me at a time when I did not believe in myself.** There is such a dearth of self-belief in our society that when a leader takes the time to truly see somebody's strengths and then communicates to them how they see those strengths, it makes a tremendous difference in that individual.

I want you to just reflect on this principle: Yesterday's dreams become today's necessities. Where have you seen that happen? Some of us were raised when there were no cell phones. Wow! The landline is almost extinct. Where else have yesterday's dreams become a today's necessity? The computer. Wow is right!

There was a time there weren't any computers when I was being raised. There was no satellite television, even before network television. Yesterday's dreams become today's necessities.

Can you think in your own life where you visualized into the future and saw something that you needed? It could even be the way you dress. It could be the way you live. It could be the present income. It could be the job. It could be the style of life. Yesterday's dreams become today's necessities. Got it? You don't want to go back.

Here's the next step. Today's dreams are tomorrow's opportunities. What you're dreaming about today will be the way tomorrow will look for you. It becomes a necessity of tomorrow. Today's dreams become tomorrow's opportunities.

If you're stuck in relationships, socially or in your business, talking about the status quo, you're stuck talking about the reality of the problems that presently exist. You are stuck talking about the way business is presently operating. If so, then tomorrow will look just like today. You caused it. It's very important to recognize that with your mind individually and collectively, you can invent a future far beyond the present reality.

This could be inside your business, inside your organization, or inside you. Those of you who are young and working your way up can contribute far beyond what is imaginable by your present status quo management. You can invent new ways, new profitable ways, new business ways, new creative ways, and new endeavors.

You can help this whole organization go far beyond where it presently is, but I know what you might be thinking. "They don't listen to me. I'm only ..." Then I would suggest that you improve your own perception of yourself, your own persuasive ability. My recommendation would be that you take on personal accountability to influence more, to influence the leadership, to help the organization become that which it's capable of becoming.

Even beyond that, you've got to help the organization see opportunity for wealth and profit. This is what the world is about — making money to support your family so you can go to dinner, so you can raise your children. You can educate them. It's all about that and you have an obligation inside that organization to be the best mind and the best employee that anybody can be. Instead of being the kind that just shows up to get the check and wait to enjoy your life outside of the organization.

What can you do to improve? You can be a genius if we can allow that genius to invent better ways. Again, I come back to, "They don't listen to me." Well, then make yourself someone they listen to. If in fact, you feel that that's not happening, do you have enough courage to start a business on your own? To move outside and get in the way instead of stopping in a negative and gloomy way inside of the culture. You would at least let the culture grow by getting out of it if you would.

I want to encourage you that the future depends upon how you're thinking now and the ability to set goals far beyond where you presently are. There is a horizon that you can see off in the distance as you look at the ocean. If you even notice that as you move toward that horizon there's another horizon? This is the way I would like to encourage you to think. There is a horizon always past the horizon but it's up to you and your imagination.

There's only one thing that you really have control over. You can't really control the future. You've lost control of the past, but you have control over the present moment. What you have control over in the present moment is the way you think.

If you think in the present moment about a better and brighter future, an improved future, you move toward it and become like what you think about. Your present thoughts do determine your future. If you can do this, your future will be exactly or quite similar to those thoughts which you are now thinking. It's not magic.

I think one of the downfalls of most people is they think they need to win the lottery to change their life, or they think that the stars need to be aligned. What I think the trap that most people fall into is they think the power over their life is outside of them, not inside of them.

Intentional living is about living a life of significance.

If you can accept the power inside yourself and activate that power by taking this knowledge and applying it to every aspect of your life, you cannot presently even imagine how your life will be. Going back to research out of Stanford University, Dr. Bandura's showed you don't let yourself want what you don't believe you can cause. What does that mean?

It means you don't let yourself dream about those things you don't think you're capable of making happen.

I could remember back when I was an Infantry Marine, the cars we had were broken down junk heaps. Every summer, my wife and I would say, "We've got to get a new car." That is exactly what we would say — "We've got to get a new car."

We didn't mean new car. We meant a new used car, a new junk heap. The idea of a new car never even entered our minds. We only thought of a used car. That was as big as we could think.

Your inner power, your belief in yourself, how your mind is, and how strong you are determine the size of your dream. As you keep developing yourself and start seeing yourself successful, the research shows your dreams get bigger and bigger.

What does the dream have to do with the way life goes? Your dream is the container with which you allow yourself to grow and develop. It's constantly important to develop what's called the efficacy inside of yourself, children, and business.

Efficacy is your belief in your own ability to make things happen, to cause, to bring about. To bring about what? To cause what? Whatever you want. Part of efficacy isn't your present knowledge base. It isn't your present money. Part of your efficacy is to know that you can know. To know that you're capable of learning. To know that you're capable of becoming or growing.

When you set a goal, you may say to yourself, "I don't know how to do it. I know. You'll learn how. I can figure it out. We'll invent the way."

If you can collectively get the people in your business or in your world around you to grow, then collectively your dreams get bigger. Collectively as an organization, you start accomplishing things that nobody in the world ever dreamed of before. You can invent your future but not with low efficacy people.

Each one of you needs to continually develop yourself and your inner strength, persistence, resilience, and ability to handle pressure and stress. All those things cause you to escalate your inner idea of who you are, your efficacy.

Your dreams get bigger, so you start taking yourself further away than 150 miles from your house and you start moving away from coaches. You start moving away from the environment. You allow yourself to move far beyond your present status quo in your normal. It's not magical. It's developmental. You can do it. Your children can do it. Your organizations can do it.

This is just the beginning. There is much more knowledge that I'm not yet sharing with you. This is only the first book. There are many books and courses that you can take but right now this is the fundamentals. You want to take and assimilate it. The follow through information and techniques that I'm giving you, and the affirmation process are not just something nice. You've got to intend to use it.

Now it isn't the knowledge you want. It isn't the affirmations that you want. It is that you want a better marriage. You want a better life. You want a better business. You want more of whatever you want. You don't need what I've got if you don't have a bigger goal. You don't need what I'm giving you if you don't want a better life.

You really don't need it, so it's of no value to you. But this is the best knowledge in the world to help you develop and change from where you are to where you want to go. In your mind, it isn't any good at all unless you apply it. So you need to start dreaming elegant dreams, big dreams, dreams that are far beyond your present normal.

What is it that I would aspire to? What do I want for myself? What do I want from my community? What do I want from my family? What do I really want to contribute to my company? What do I want to contribute to my county? What can I do? Who can I be? I'm so small. Then get bigger. I'm so incapable. Then get capable.

You can start like I started and the journey is a wonderful journey. It's a journey that is a fulfilling journey. It's inspiring. Every day is a party. Every day is exciting. Work is fun. Contribution is fun. My life is fun. How did it get fun? I caused it. I caused it and so can you.

Stay tuned, I'm going to teach you how. As you have now read this book entirely I guess now is a good time as any to share with you about our Today-Is-the-Day Workshops where I vividly present the concepts and education in-person. I provide more of the revealing and productive insights into how you think and how your thoughts affect how you act.

The tools and techniques we teach are easily recognizable stories and examples that can be applied immediately to help you reach your goals easily and enjoyably. Life is propelled out of the ordinary and into an exciting adventure. You can learn more about our workshops on the Today Is the Day website: www.todayisthedaybook.com/workshops

Answer the following POWERFUL LIFE CHANGING QUESTIONS:

Grow from the Comfort-Zone

1. What perceptions of myself need to change in order for me to reach my goals?

_____

_____

_____

_____

_____

_____

_____

_____

_____

_____

_____

_____

_____

_____

2. What parts of my life and work do I not want to change?

_____
_____
_____
_____
_____
_____
_____
_____
_____
_____
_____
_____
_____
_____

3. What are my horizons beyond this horizon that I can see right now? What affirmations do I need to create in order to keep that horizon in focus?

_____
_____
_____
_____
_____
_____
_____
_____
_____
_____
_____
_____
_____
_____

My Notes:

_____
_____
_____
_____
_____
_____
_____
_____
_____
_____
_____
_____
_____
_____
_____
_____
_____
_____
_____
_____

If you haven't as yet done so, I implore you to take an internal inventory now of where you are. Work on changing or improving. That starts with answering the questions and taking your notes about what came up for you while reading this entire book. If it's hard to accept where you are, there is always hope, and you can change. That's exactly why you got this BOOK, RIGHT?

So make the change by starting NOW! Go back through the book, especially if you skipped over the questions and fill them in. When you attend one of our live Today Is the Day workshops, we go through each question in depth, and I personally hold you accountable before moving on. So even though I'm not there reading with you personally, pretend I'm there now holding you accountable.

Take great comfort in knowing that ALL great feats are accomplished one small step at a time. TAKE THE SMALL STEPS!

They make a BIG difference. I would love to know how it worked for you; I enjoy the comments on my Facebook page (FB.com/obombowen), and I look forward to hearing from you soon.

This is probably the simplest way I can help you remain accountable to your continued growth and success. If you're more hands on like my wife, then join us at one of our upcoming workshops. If you're ready to learn how to transform your life, success, or marriage, join the next Today Is the Day workshop, the best life-transforming program.

For more information, go to www.todayisthedaybook.com and give yourself this gift as a reward of investing in your happiness and growth. The greatest gift my wife and I have ever given ourselves is attending 4 growth and leadership and marriage retreats per year since 2010. We still do it to this day; you can never stop growing or investing in yourself.

THANK YOU!

You've reached the end and have now POSSIBLY for the first time PROVEN to yourself that you are worth it. When Ana and I first learned this information, we could not believe how many people just like us were living an unsatisfied life.

We are truly happy that you decided to invest in yourself and create a POSITIVE Change with us in the world. You are now an AMBASSADOR of this information with us. Our goal is to influence a POSITIVE change in the world, by getting this information into the hands of and changing the lives of one billion other human beings.

As a new AMBASSADOR, you can now help yourself and us with this goal. Here's how. Get five friends or family members who you will share what you've learned in this book. Simply ask them to help keep you accountable with your goals moving forward.

My 5 Accountability Partners Are:

1. _____
2. _____
3. _____
4. _____
5. _____

ABOUT THE AUTHOR

Obom Bowen is a retired, decorated Marine who, as an Infantry Commander, received the Purple Heart for his service and wounds sustained in combat. Hailing from very humble beginnings, Obom has achieved success as a Master Career Strategist and a consummate entrepreneur who has a passion for studying human behavior, personal development, psychology, philosophy, and creating strategies that work.

His expertise has helped Fortune 500 companies, including Chevron, Wal-Mart stores, Walgreens, Intel and others. His expertise in helping individuals achieve business and life success has landed him in collaborations with: *Success from Home* magazine 2012, 2013, 2014, and 2015: Knightscove Media Corp: A multi-national social media company, and Heidi Lerner author of *Grey Matters*.

Obom has been seen on Fox News, KUSN, SIGN ON San Diego, featured in Top Coastal news, *Union Tribune* and has spoken and taught as a Facilitator for NVTSI, Reboot and at a number of colleges and university (i.e. UCLA, UCSD, Central Texas College).

Today, Obom is Founder and CEO of Global Fairy Tale and Today Is the Day, where Making Relationships Better through Believing and Achieving in Each Other is their founding principle. Every marriage is unique, expressed by the colorful personalities of each spouse and textured by the circumstances at play in their lives. Blending these is a divinely inspired art form from challenging to mastery, but definitely worth the effort.

Obom has a passion for helping individuals break through psychological barriers that hold them back. He has developed unique strategies for confidence building, career coaching, executive coaching, and strategic consulting, including personal development initiatives, life coaching, helping organizations and companies building cohesion culture, production, corporate training and development with an overall goal of reduced cost and increased profits.

Obom is also the International Award Winning Best-selling author of, *The Philosophy of Success* and *Passion 365*.

"Obom Bowen has masterfully used a journey of words mixed with his life experiences to help us recognize the well-spring of potential that exists within each of us and show us a better way of being who we are truly meant to be." David Byrd, CEO and Founder of David Byrd Consulting, LLC and Author of *The Tripping Point in Leadership*

Contact Obom Directly: obom@todayisthedaybook.com

CONTINUE YOUR JOURNEY

Join the Today Is the Day movement …

Today Is the Day Workshop:

The Today Is the Day education provides tools that become lasting resources to foster love, happiness, success, and fulfillment. This workshop is the foundation's flagship program. It's designed to create positive, enduring shifts in the quality and resilience of marriages, families, and business relationships. Our research-validated training delivered over an intensive weekend or consecutive weekly sessions, introduces essential skills for improving communication, self-worth, empathy, emotional expression, and healthy conflict resolution on the behalf of lasting breakthroughs in work, business, and relationship satisfaction. REGISTER NOW: www.todayisthedaybook.com

Today Is The Day Home Study Course:

Vividly presenting the concepts and education virtually, Obom Bowen provides revealing and productive insights into how you think and how your thoughts affect how you act. The tools and techniques Obom teaches in easily recognizable stories and examples can be applied immediately to help you reach your goals easily and enjoyably. Life is propelled out of the ordinary into the extraordinary.

The foundation of all human action is human thought. Our thought process forms the foundation on which we build every facet of our lives. Therefore, it is important for each of us to understand how our minds work – how we got the habits and attitudes, the beliefs that may stand in the way of releasing our vast inner potential and leading fulfilling and purposeful lives. Our beliefs and expectations about ourselves, our families, our organizations – indeed, our world – are directly reflected in our "performance reality." The Today Is the Day home study course will teach you how to effectively change your current "performance reality."

REGISTER NOW: www.todayisthedaybook.com

We hope you enjoy this book from Obom Bowen. Our goal is to provide high-quality, thought provoking books and products that connect truth to your real needs and challenges. For more information on other books and products that will help you with all your important needs, go to www.todayisthedaybook.com

www.todayisthedaybook.com